CHRISTIANITY AND WESTERN THEISM

This book explores central philosophical questions in Christian theology and doctrine through the perspectives of three of the most influential Christian thinkers: St. Augustine, St. Anselm, and St. Thomas Aquinas.

Chapters analyze long-contested debates around the Trinity, Original Sin, the Incarnation, Grace, Divine Foreknowledge and Free Will, the Afterlife, and Christian Exclusivity. From these topics emerge the "hard questions":

- How are ideas of monotheism and the Trinity reconciled?
- Is the doctrine of the Incarnation coherent?
- Why does God give grace to some and not others?
- How can the afterlife be understood?
- How should non-Christians be treated?

Through a compelling comparative investigation of these ideas, *Christianity and Western Theism* uses the enduring concepts of three towering philosophers to show that Christian doctrine, though difficult, is coherent and, to some extent, understandable.

As an engaging and accessible introduction to this topic, this book is the ideal resource for new students of Christian thought, Christian philosophy, philosophy of religion, and medieval philosophy.

Katherin A. Rogers is a professor of philosophy, University of Delaware, USA.

CHRISTIANITY AND WESTERN THEISM

Classical Approaches to the Hard Questions

Katherin A. Rogers

Routledge
Taylor & Francis Group

LONDON AND NEW YORK

Designed cover image: Getty – AVTG

First published 2024
by Routledge
4 Park Square, Milton Park, Abingdon, Oxon OX14 4RN

and by Routledge
605 Third Avenue, New York, NY 10158

*Routledge is an imprint of the Taylor & Francis Group, an informa
business*

British Library Cataloguing-in-Publication Data
A catalogue record for this book is available from the British Library

ISBN: 978-1-032-06398-0 (hbk)
ISBN: 978-1-032-06399-7 (pbk)
ISBN: 978-1-003-20208-0 (ebk)

DOI: 10.4324/9781003202080

Typeset in ITC Galliard Pro
by KnowledgeWorks Global Ltd.

CONTENTS

ACKNOWLEDGMENTS

I would like to thank Prof. Jeremy Skrzypek for his generous help. It is a better book due to his thoughtful comments on each chapter.

INTRODUCTION

The core beliefs that distinguish Christianity from other monotheisms are intellectually challenging. The present book is an introduction to how three great Christian philosophers, St. Augustine of Hippo (354–430 CE), St. Anselm of Canterbury (1033–1109 CE), and St. Thomas Aquinas (1225–1274 CE) address some of these core beliefs such as the Trinity and the Incarnation. Some of these beliefs are set forth in early creeds from the "ecumenical" councils accepted by most Christians. Some, such as the doctrines of original sin and the necessity of grace, are hammered out by the Church Fathers, especially Augustine. Augustine, Anselm, and Aquinas (AAA, for brevity's sake) take all of the core claims to be based on Scripture, and most cannot be demonstrated philosophically. They are revealed truths to be accepted on faith. The role of philosophy is to address the "hard questions" and show that the core claims are coherent. They do not violate the laws of logic, and they are understandable, up to a point. The modest goal of the present book is to explain some of the hard questions, show why they are "hard", and outline ways AAA suggest to mitigate the difficulties.

AAA all embrace what can be called "Classical Theism". In that Augustine and Anselm represent an approach influenced by Neoplatonism, while Aquinas works within a more Aristotelian framework, focusing on these three shows how two main philosophical currents from antiquity inform Christian thought on the hard questions.[1] An uncountable number of volumes have been written about these issues and about AAA, but in order to offer a concise introduction I have limited references almost exclusively to texts by AAA. The reader unused to accessing the work of late classical and medieval authors might find the citations confusing, so I include a short guide on how to understand them at the end of this introduction before the "Outline of the Book". The bibliography lists readily available English translations.

DOI: 10.4324/9781003202080-1

In this introductory chapter I sketch some preliminaries. First I review how AAA understand the basic nature of God and God's relationship to the universe. Having emphasized the transcendence and unlimitedness of God, the question arises: How can our limited terms and concepts be used to talk about Him? AAA all hold that we can talk positively and meaningfully about God, but there is disagreement concerning what we can properly mean. I will then say a little about how AAA interpret Scripture. A brief discussion of the early Church Councils follows and then a defense of the reasonableness of believing some things on faith. The hard questions we are addressing involve the miraculous, and so a note on how AAA view miracles is in order. The Introduction concludes with a note on how to understand the citations and a brief outline of the chapters in the book.

The Nature of God

Although AAA do not march in lock step regarding the nature of God, their views are similar enough to allow for a basic sketch. The outline will be enough to proceed with the hard questions. AAA take God to be "that than which no greater can be conceived". (This is Anselm's description at the beginning of his *Proslogion*. The rest of the book unpacks the phrase.) "Greater" here means better in every way in which it is possible to be great; not great relative to some limiting category, like a great car, but simply great with no limitations and all perfections. If we were thinking of some being X, and then realized we could think of a greater being, Y, we would know that X is not God. This approach is today called "Perfect Being Theology" (PBT). This is not to say that we can fully comprehend or grasp how God is in Himself. God is greater than we can conceive. Which is not surprising. God is the source of all, and we are radically limited creatures. If you and I could paint a complete and accurate conceptual picture of some being X, we would know that X is not God.

Why start with PBT? Religious reasons include that there are scriptural passages pointing out the ultimate greatness of God and insisting that God alone is to be worshipped. But if you and I, with our radically limited cognitive apparatus, could think of a better being than God, then the god we have in mind would have to be a very small divinity and hardly worthy of worship. Furthermore, believers in God agree that He is the creator of our world. AAA argue that as the creator God must possess, in a perfect way, the good reflected in created things, but must transcend all the limiting categories of creation. It is this perfect and unlimited God that PBT hopes to capture. Philosophers disagree about what attributes are entailed by perfect "greatness". Many contemporary philosophers of religion reject attributes that AAA take to be fundamental. There is some disagreement even among AAA, but there is much more agreement than disagreement. When their views differ in ways that are relevant to the "hard questions" the differences will be noted.

Most Christian philosophers, past and present, have agreed on three key divine attributes; God is omnipotent (all-powerful), omniscient (all-knowing), and perfectly good. There has been, and continues to be, debate about how to understand these attributes, but AAA offer views that are similar enough for a rough outline. The most fundamental exercise of divine power is God's making everything (besides Himself) to exist *ex nihilo* (from nothing) and keeping all that exists in being from moment to moment. For AAA these are not two separate creative activities of God. God is "creating" all the time in that, if God were to stop willing the existence of some creature right now, it would blink out of being. Aquinas points out that even if the past were infinite, we would still require God as the cause of there being something rather than nothing.[2] Can God make a round-square? No. A round-square is a logical impossibility, something that is A and not-A in the same way at the same time, and even God does not do the logically impossible. Couldn't an omnipotent being be above the laws of logic? Maybe He *decided* upon them and cannot be bound by them? No. If logic does not apply to God then God might be A and not-A in the same way at the same time – strong and weak, good and bad. Then nothing meaningful could be said about God. Christians have a Scripture and worship practices which require that they are able to think about God coherently, if in a limited way. AAA agree that God does not violate the laws of logic. Are there, then, rules of logic existing independently of God to which He has to conform? No, say AAA. God makes everything that is not Himself including whatever properties and principles can be said to exist. There is nothing outside of God and His activity, not even the laws of logic. Rather, our discipline of logic spells out the rules for thinking correctly about reality – God and all the creatures He has made or could make – creatures which are reflections of the divine nature. The rules of logic grow out of the divine will and divine nature (which are actually the same, as we will see).[3]

Besides the logically impossible, there are many more things that God cannot do because they can only be done by limited creatures. You might stub your toe, but God (setting aside the Incarnation for now) is incorporeal and so He has no toes to stub. You might forget what you had for dinner last night, but God cannot forget. You might struggle to learn Latin, but God does not make an effort. The list goes on and on. For AAA the most useful definition of "omnipotence" is that it is the power to do anything logically possible for a perfect and unlimited being.

Can God do something wicked? No, say AAA. Are there moral principles existing independently of God which He perfectly obeys? Of course not. God is the source of everything not Himself. Does God, then, decide on the moral principles such that the good action is whatever God commands and God could command anything logically possible? This is known today as "Divine Command Theory". Late in the Middle Ages some philosophers – William of Ockham is a prime example – adopt this position. But AAA hold that moral principles are aimed at the flourishing of the human being. They flow inevitably out of human nature, and human nature is a product of the divine will.[4] More fundamentally, moral principles are a subset of a deeper value. Everything that exists is good just in that it is an existent being. We could label this "ontological" value – meaning related to being or existence. At the beginning of Genesis God sees that *all* the things He has made are good, not just the human beings. If you doubt God's interest in the whole of His creation, look at the Book of Job where God enumerates many of the magnificent things He has made that exist entirely outside the paths of human commerce.[5] God Himself is the ultimate existent Who shares His being with the rest of creation. As with the laws of logic, the principles of morality are not a set of rules external to God, nor does He decide upon them arbitrarily. Rather they are rooted in God's will and nature. God is Himself the *standard* for all value. Created things are better or less good, ontologically as well as morally, as they reflect the nature of God. (What of evil? Evil is a lack, or perversion, or corruption, or destruction of some good. It has no ontological status in itself. It is parasitic through and through.[6])

AAA agree that it is incoherent to suppose that God could do something wrong. But does God inevitably do what is *best*? All three say, "Yes", in that God's activity is perfect. But could this perfect divine activity issue in a different creation, or no creation at all? Here there is disagreement. AAA all say that God is free. He is a rational agent Who does what He does by will. But "divine freedom" has somewhat different meanings for the three philosophers. Augustine and Anselm (as I read them) hold that God, being perfectly good, acts for the best, and could not do otherwise than He does. For example, He could not fail to create, and He could not fail to create the world He has actually made. But He is free since His will is not restricted by anything. As the source of all, He exists in absolute independence of anything else and so He possesses the most perfect freedom. His goodness is not something outside of Himself, and it is unreasonable to hold that willing in accord with His nature is limiting for God.[7] Aquinas disagrees: Divine freedom requires that God could have done other than He has done. He might have created a different world, or not created at all.[8] This disagreement has consequences regarding some of the hard questions. For example, did God *have to* respond to original sin the way He did?

The third attribute to consider is omniscience. AAA agree that God knows everything about everything. Indeed, God's knowing and His causing things to exist is ultimately the same thing for AAA. So saying that "God has beliefs..." about this or that is not the right locution. Divine omniscience is an immediate "presence" of things to God. AAA agree that God knows all there is to know about the past, the present, and the future. This raises the puzzle of how God can foreknow future human choices if those choices are really free. AAA propose differing solutions as we will see in Chapter Five. But that God does know the future is not open to question. Scripture and Church tradition endorse the claim. Divine sovereignty demands it, and it is entailed by Perfect Being Theology. PBT requires that God is that than which no greater can be conceived. If God knew only the past and the present, we could conceive of a being which is greater, a being that also knows the future.[9]

Most philosophers of religion, past and present, are committed to God's being omnipotent, omniscient, and perfectly good, though contemporary philosophers often understand these terms very differently from AAA. But AAA were equally committed to several more divine attributes which contemporary philosophers often reject. These include divine simplicity, immutability, impassibility, and eternality. AAA argue that God is simple, since anything composed of parts is dependent upon those parts. God cannot be dependent on anything.[10] Moreover, something composed of parts can be decomposed – even if only conceptually. If God is that than which no greater can be conceived, then He cannot even be *thought* to pass out of being. So God must be simple.[11] We have been speaking of God having *attributes* in the plural. From our human perspective, we sometimes have to speak this way, but this is strictly incorrect on two counts. First, we should not separate God's nature or self from the attributes. God does not *have* or *possesses* power or knowledge or goodness. God simply *is* His omnipotence, omniscience, and goodness. And secondly, these attributes (since we must use the term) are really all the same and are identical to God's nature. God's power is the same thing as His knowledge which is the same thing as His goodness. AAA go so far as to hold that God cannot be separated from His activities – actor and act are the same. God knows all He knows and does all He does in one, simple, act which is identical to His nature.[12] Philosophically this is a difficult doctrine, and trying to render it consistent with core Christian teachings adds a new level of difficulty. How can a simple God be a Trinity? And how can only one person of the Trinity become incarnate? AAA offer analyses that avoid logical contradiction, even if they do not allow us to fully comprehend how God can be simple and triune. AAA insist that it is a mistake to believe that the finite human mind is capable of spelling out the nature of God with analytic clarity. A being we could wrap our minds around just would not be God. If we can achieve a glimpse of the divine, however dim and distant, we should be grateful.

Immutability is another attribute which AAA ascribe to God. As a perfect, simple act nothing could be added to or taken away from God.[13] We should even deny that God knows and does different things at different times since that would entail the multiplicity of a constant divine nature underlying, and separate from, the changing knowings and doings. How can an immutable God interact with a changing world? The question, raised by Augustine, requires a look at the nature of time (an issue that will arise again in Chapter Five). Augustine meditates on the nature of time in his *Confessions*, Book 11, but scholars debate his conclusions. For our purposes, there are roughly two main theories of time. "Presentism" (these are contemporary terms) is the view that only the present moment exists. The past and future are nonexistent. "Isotemporalism" (sometimes called "four-dimensionalism" or "eternalism") holds that all times exist equally. What we call past, present, and future are equally real, and what counts as past or present or future is relative to a given perceiver at a given time. On presentism, it is difficult to see how God could be immutable. AAA take it that God knows and acts immediately upon His creation. He is willing what exists right now to exist right now. But then it seems that – on presentism – what He knows and does must change from moment to moment. Aquinas – whose position on time is debatable – holds that God knows all that he knows and does all that He does without there being any change in Him. God's activity remains exactly the same whatever changes creatures undergo. God's activity would be exactly the same even if He had chosen not to create. This is a puzzling position. Some connect this to Aquinas's thesis that, while creatures are really related to God, God is not really related to creatures. They take this to mean that whenever we say that God knows or does something with regard to creatures, we are really speaking about the creatures, not about any knowledge or activity in God.[14]

As I read him Anselm offers an isotemporalist solution to the dilemma of an immutable God knowing and acting on a changing world. All of time is equally real and is immediately present to God. God can know and do all He knows and does in one immutable act because all of reality – including what we call past, present, and future – is there for Him at once.[15] AAA understand the divine attribute of eternality – divine timelessness – as at least the thought that God has always existed, will always exist, and is not affected by the passage of time. On presentism

God exists at every moment of time, but immutably. And, again, it is hard to square this with God knowingly sustaining a changing world in being from moment to moment. But if time is isotemporal, then divine eternality means that God is not "stretched out" along time in any way at all, but all times are equally real and immediately "there" for God.

The way AAA understand divine omnipotence requires that God be impassible, that is, He cannot be affected by things outside Himself, and He cannot experience emotions as we do. God is the source of everything with ontological status so the arrow of causation must run from God to creation and cannot run the other way. And (bracketing the Incarnation for now) God does not feel sorrow or anger or fear, etc. As human emotions, these are tied to the body. God in Himself does not have a body. More fundamentally, nothing can budge God off of His perfect state of love and joy.[16] If we understand the divine condition to be one of only positive, infinite happiness then perhaps we could say that God does experience an emotion. But when we use a term like "divine happiness" we can grasp only a dim reflection of that "emotion". Divine happiness far transcends even the most extreme and complete human happiness. (The question of what sort of emotions we should ascribe to Christ incarnate will be addressed in Chapter Three.)

How do AAA understand God as Creator? In the Middle Ages God's causing things to exist *ex nihilo* is "primary causation", while the created system of creaturely causes and effects is "secondary causation". Some philosophers, past and present, have supposed that there is *only* primary causation. They have taken it that this enhances divine omnipotence. Absolutely everything that exists and happens is immediately caused by God and is not also caused by anything else. Today this view is known as "Occasionalism"; on the occasion of A – what we mistakenly take to be a cause – God subsequently makes B happen. But that B follows A does not prove that A causes B. AAA reject this approach. Occasionalism had not been proposed in Augustine's time, or in Anselm's, but it is fair to say that, although they do not use the labels "primary" and "secondary" causation, they assume that created things express causal powers while all of creation is kept in being by the immediate will of God. Aquinas, writing after some Islamic philosophers had proposed it, explicitly argues against Occasionalism. God creates excellent creatures, and a being that can exercise and receive causal power is just a better kind of thing than one that cannot.[17] (Indeed, how could something exist at all absent its active and passive causal powers?) A related assumption is that God wants there to be lots of wonderful kinds of creatures. Augustine and Anselm, as I read them, subscribe to a strong version of the "Principle of Plenitude". God creates as many different kinds of beings as He can, since it is a better world with all those creatures in it.[18] God, of course, is keeping all the beings in existence with all of their powers and actions.

AAA take it that God deeply values secondary causation. He values it in the case of individual creatures, and He values the causal system of the universe as a whole. This is directly relevant to the problem of evil. For example, if God wanted there to be human beings, why would He have us evolve from earlier animals, with all the pain and suffering that that process required? Why not just "poof!" us into being? The obvious answer, as every school child knows, is that dinosaurs and other prehistoric fauna and flora are really great. They are great in themselves, and they are great as part of the overall causal system of the universe. Yes, there is pain and suffering, but it is worth this cost to have all the marvelous creatures that we are blessed with.[19] This rejection of Occasionalism and positing a divine commitment to secondary causation plays out in interesting ways when we address the hard questions. Rather than the bizarre rigmarole of the Incarnation, why doesn't God just say "poof!" everybody is saved (or those He chooses to be saved are saved)? Or, if God wants to incarnate, why go through the process of Mary conceiving and giving birth? Why not just produce Jesus, full grown, from behind a rock in the vicinity of Jerusalem? At least part of the answer is that God values secondary causation. (This will be relevant to how AAA assess the miraculous.)

Finally, AAA take it that God is "personal" in two ways. He is a person, a rational free agent. Though (as we will see in Chapter One) they make it clear that "person" in discussing the Trinity is used in a very unusual and special way. Further, God is personal in that He takes an interest in, and has a plan for, each of us.[20] Given how many of us there are just on planet earth, is this hard to envision? Certainly! I cannot even make an adequate picture of God's relationship to everyone in Los Angeles. AAA respond that no one is required to produce an imagining of God's personal presence to everyone and everything. Our job is to love God, to love our neighbors as ourselves, to recognize our failings, to pray hard, and keep up our hope. The effort to address the hard questions – in however dim and distant a way – is part of the job.

Talking about God

God is a being greater than we can conceive. Human beings are radically limited in our natures, and our life experiences occupy only a tiny bit of time and space. How can our words and concepts possibly be used properly of God? One approach is to say that we can't talk or think about God and should shut up right now. Some earlier theists, such as Plotinus (204/5–270 CE), the most important non-Christian Neoplatonist, offered that advice. But Christians (and Jews and Muslims) cannot go that route. Christians have a Scripture that offers positive descriptions of God and worship practices that require talking to and about God. The words and concepts we use of God are surely not just meaningless or utterly mistaken.

AAA hold that human beings can talk and think meaningfully about God. But there is a difference between the approach of Augustine and Anselm on the one hand and Aquinas on the other. All agree that words and concepts like "good" and "wise" can be applied to both creatures and God with positive meaning. The issue is *how* these words apply across the Creator/creature divide. For our purposes there are basically two positive ways. (An important "negative way" will also be mentioned.) Our words apply to God and to creatures either univocally or equivocally. "Univocally" means that a word can be applied to God and creatures with the same meaning – though perhaps with significant qualifications. Augustine does not offer a developed analysis of how language is used of God and creatures, but his follower, Anselm, argues for a version of univocity. "Equivocally" means that our words have different meanings when applied to God and to creatures. Aquinas holds that our words apply equivocally, but not *purely* equivocally. Pure equivocation would entail that the meanings of words when used of God and creatures are altogether different so that we cannot think or speak meaningfully about God. Aquinas explains that our words apply "analogically". The meaning is different, but related. (Using language "analogically" is not the same as proposing analogies in discussing things divine, as we will see.)

A fundamental motivation for this difference of opinion is rooted in AAA's differing analyses of two related questions: "What is the relationship between God and creatures?" and "How is human knowledge possible?" For the more Platonic Augustine and Anselm creation "participates" in God; that is, created things reflect divine ideas and are caused so immediately by God that we can speak of creatures "sharing in" the divine nature. Anselm makes this clear when he is talking about Justice and about Truth. At the beginning of his *Monologion* he offers a Platonic proof for the existence of God: We recognize many just things, but all just things are just by sharing in justice, and God is the Justice in which all other just things share. Similarly with truth. In *On Truth* he says that there are many different true things (The truth of statements is only one kind among many.) which are all true by participating in the Highest Truth, God.

Both Augustine and Anselm hold that human knowledge requires access to divine ideas and both accept the doctrine of divine illumination: When the mind is prepared to receive certain knowledge, God "shines" it into the mind. How else could one grasp truths that are not contained in the physical world and could not be delivered by the senses? Take $3 + 7 = 10$. As Augustine explains in Book 2 of *On Free Will*, $3 + 7 = 10$ is not a fact about bodies. The physical world changes, but $3 + 7 = 10$ does not. If the physical world ceased to exist, $3 + 7$ would still $= 10$. If you know that $3 + 7 = 10$ at all, then you know that it is true always and everywhere. But no one's senses reach to always and everywhere. $3 + 7 = 10$ is an eternal and immutable truth. And it is superior to the human mind in that, if your reasoning disagrees with $3 + 7 = 10$, it is not $3 + 7 = 10$ which must change to conform to your mind, but the reverse. Truth with a capital "T", of which the necessary truths of mathematics are an aspect, can be identified with God. And – back to participation – the created universe is made up of things with forms (natures, essences), which depend upon mathematics.

In Book 2 of *On Free Will*, Augustine is also concerned with "Wisdom", truths about values. Wisdom, too, is an aspect of Truth i.e. God. Our created universe is imbued not only with mathematical principles, but with value – all being is good according to Augustine. And recognizing value requires divine illumination. Augustine holds that this is easily seen with certain moral principles, such as fundamental principles of justice – for example, equals must be treated equally – which are the same always and everywhere. But justice is not a sensible quality. In order to recognize basic truths we must receive that light of divine illumination.[21]

The doctrines of participation and divine illumination require that created things exhibit a "sameness" with God, in whose being they share, and that human knowers appreciate this sameness through illumination. It is not surprising to find Augustine more or less assuming that our language can apply to God univocally. Anselm spells it out clearly, especially when he defines "justice" and "freedom". Both God and human agents can be just and free. But aren't God and human agents so different that the terms can't mean the same thing when applied to both? It is true, says Anselm, that God just *is* the Justice in which all just things share. And human freedom plays out differently from divine freedom. Yet Anselm holds that if we use the same terms of God and creatures, we must offer definitions that can cover both of these very different kinds of beings. There must be an underlying sameness, univocity, in order for us to speak and think meaningfully about God.[22]

Aquinas emphasizes participation less than do his more Neoplatonic predecessors. (He does use the word, and scholars debate the extent to which he has departed from the earlier Neoplatonism.) And, following Aristotle, he is an empiricist in his epistemology; our natural knowledge begins with experience, mainly sense experience. For Augustine and Anselm you cannot answer the question of how anyone knows anything without invoking the immediate presence and causal activity of God on the human knower through divine illumination. And certainly, for Aquinas, you cannot *fully* answer the question of how anyone knows anything without appealing to God. God is the rational designer who made the human cognitive faculties to work as they do. However, you can answer the epistemic question of how we know things without bringing God into the picture. On Aquinas's view, the human knower gathers information from the senses, and the mind processes that information to pick out what is essential. That is how we grasp the natures of things – like the catness of the cat – even though we are confronted with only individual cats, each of which appears different to our senses. And even the truths of mathematics and value can be "abstracted" from the data delivered by observation.[23]

This empiricist epistemology puts Aquinas in an especially difficult position regarding how our language applies to God. Our concepts are derived from things in the physical world which are limited and caused. Moreover, these things only *have* certain properties. This man may have goodness and wisdom, but these properties are added to his human nature and are changeable. As immutable and simple God just *is* Goodness and Wisdom, the source and standard for all that is good and wise. God's goodness and wisdom are one and the same and identical with His nature. Thus, according to Aquinas, the terms we apply to God must mean something different than when we apply them to the creatures from which we learned them. *Pure* equivocation would entail that the terms we gathered from observing creatures would not have any meaning for us when we apply them to God. That cannot be right, says Aquinas. So he adopts the doctrine of analogy.[24]

Scholars debate about how Aquinas's doctrine of analogy should be spelled out. He gives us an example, from Aristotle, which is useful up to a point. Take the term "healthy". Its primary use refers to a healthy animal, say a healthy horse. But there are other uses. The veterinarian might tell you that the horse's urine is healthy, or this medicine is healthy, or that exercise is healthy. None of those other three uses means the same as "healthy" when talking about the healthy body. "Healthy" is used analogously. The four meanings are different, but related, with the last three referring back to the primary meaning – the healthy body. And so with language about God. The term "good" for example, may be used of God, of a human being, of a book, of an action. All four meanings are somewhat different. They are related, says Aquinas, because God is the primary Good, the source and standard of all the good things. But although God is primary in reality, from our perspective – in the order of our knowledge – creatures are primary. That is, we grasp the meaning of the term by observing creatures and then apply it to God.[25]

However, if the meanings of terms are derived from creatures, can we really move to saying anything meaningful of God? With Aquinas's example of "healthy", if you did not already grasp what health in a body meant, the veterinarian's other three uses of "healthy" would not have meaning for you. In the case of "healthy" you need to know the primary meaning first in order to grasp the secondary meanings. Some scholars interpret Aquinas's doctrine of analogy as meant to keep us at a distance from God, to have little, if any, concept of God in Himself. An alternative is to emphasize Aquinas's argument in the Fourth Way that the goods in creatures preexist in God[26] and to say that, although our terms do not mean the same thing when applied to God and creatures, still there is a thin thread of univocity. For example, since all goodness is rooted in God, it is on some level the same goodness that God is infinitely and causally and that creatures have as caused and finite...at least it is similar enough that when we say that God is supremely good, we are truly talking about God and understanding something positive by what we say.

There are volumes and volumes written debating Aquinas's doctrine of analogy. Here I will take it that AAA allow some univocity in how our language applies to God. But lest this tempt the human knower to think he can comprehend or "wrap his mind around" God, note that AAA unanimously appeal at times to a *via negativa*, a negative way to speak of God. There are different versions of the *via negativa* in the Middle Ages, but we can attribute to AAA a version which is a qualification of the acceptance of univocal language, rather than a simple contradiction of it. Yes, God is, for example, good and wise with a goodness and a wisdom not entirely dissimilar to human goodness and wisdom. But God is *so* good and *so* wise that our limited concepts of goodness and wisdom just cannot capture the divine nature. It is appropriate, then, to say that God is not-good and not-wise. Not that God is bad or stupid! Rather, the human mind cannot grasp the extent of the goodness and wisdom in God. The analogy that is often used is drawn from the sun and its light. The Medievals had the (mistaken, sadly) idea that the sun poured forth its light, essentially the same thing as itself, without ever being diminished. The light falling on the objects around us is sunlight, and it enables us to see, but we dare not gaze upon the sun itself. If we try, we will be blinded. We will see only darkness. This is not because the sun is not bright, but because it is *so* bright that our limited vision fails.[27] Accepting some univocity, qualified by the *via negativa*, allows us to hold that we can speak and think of God meaningfully without supposing that we can fully grasp the divine nature.[28]

AAA take the existence and basic nature of God to be demonstrable through reason. Those with the time and talent to engage in philosophy do not need faith or revelation to see that the God of PBT exists. But there is a further difficulty to be addressed. The present book deals with the "hard questions" of Christianity, doctrines often revealed in Scripture and Church teaching. Omnipotence and omniscience and divine goodness are difficult enough, but the specifically Christian doctrines – like the Trinity and the Incarnation – are even harder. How can God be three persons in one nature? How can Christ be two natures in one person? AAA hold that even if Christians cannot understand these doctrines, they must accept them.[29] But AAA agree that we can take steps toward understanding. First, they work to spell out these doctrines in a way that does not involve contradiction. Maybe we cannot construct a clear picture in our minds, but we can see that no fundamental incoherence is involved. And we can do even a bit better. AAA take it that analogies drawn from creatures can help us catch a glimpse of the triune and incarnate God. For example, as we will see in Chapter One, Augustine spells out an analogy for the Trinity, drawn from the human mind. And they use analogies to deal with other hard questions like original sin and bodily resurrection. While we are pilgrims in this world, we must not expect to see God face to face, but His images are everywhere to guide us on the journey to Him.

Interpreting Scripture

In the present work we will not be canvassing Scriptural passages relevant to the hard questions we are considering. (Augustine and Aquinas have both done that job for us with amazing thoroughness.) But it is useful to say a word about how AAA approach the Bible. AAA hold that Scripture is the inerrant word of God. Augustine, setting the tone for most subsequent medieval intellectuals, argues that it should be taken "literally", but "literally" does not mean that it must be taken in whatever meaning first leaps out at you. "Literally" means in the sense that the divinely inspired author intends. Augustine's discussion of the first books of Genesis makes this clear. God is said to create in a series of "days", but "days" cannot mean what we ordinarily mean by the word – the twenty-four hour period from sunrise to sunrise or the time from sunrise to sunset. The sun is not created until the fourth day. Augustine tentatively suggests that the "days" are moments in the angelic consciousness, where the angels – the first-created "light" – occupy a mid-point between time and eternity.[30] Regarding the physical universe Augustine borrows the Stoic notion of "seminal reasons". In the beginning God implanted the "seed-like" potencies for things that would unfold over time.[31] How much time? Impossible to say. Augustine's "literal" reading of Genesis is, coincidentally, easy to square with the theory of evolution, as long as God is the primary cause of the secondary causes at work. (Augustine offers a timely chapter on the mistake of thinking that the Bible is a textbook in the physical sciences.[32])

Augustine holds that biblical interpretation is difficult. There are multiple layers of meaning to be discovered.[33] It requires effort, time, intelligence, and education. Further, it must be done within the community of the Church by one with a commitment to the teachings of the Church. AAA all share this approach and could not accept the thought that each individual should crack open the Good Book and decide for himself what it means.

Three main principles of Scriptural interpretation that AAA assume should be noted. In that the *whole* Bible is inerrant, if we come across passages *here* that suggest one claim and *there* that suggest the denial of the claim, we know that these initial "suggestions" need to be interpreted so as not to conflict. Logical impossibilities do not happen. Secondly, if there are passages that seem at odds with the statements of the Church Councils, again interpretation is in order. (Augustine is writing after the Council of Nicaea, but before the Council of Chalcedon, and sometimes we find him appealing to the "right rule of faith" – presumably what he took to be the authoritative teaching of the Church.) Finally, any biblical claim that seems to diminish God needs interpretation. If, at first glance, the Bible seems to say that God makes mistakes, forgets things, acts out of arbitrary anger, etc. then these passages must be understood in a way that conforms to PBT.[34] (We might add a fourth, overarching principle. Augustine spells it out in the first book of *On Christian Doctrine*, and Anselm and Aquinas would certainly agree: We must approach Scripture in a spirit of charity, that is, we must take the text to be urging us on to love of God and love of neighbor.)

Importance of the Councils

As recorded in the Gospels Jesus gathered many followers and taught them. The Acts of the Apostles goes on to describe how more and more followers were added as Christianity took hold. But quickly disputes arose on a variety of issues, practical and doctrinal. We see in Acts the beginnings of the methodology the Christian community adopted to settle disputes. Some of these disputes arose because the original followers of Jesus were Jews, obeying the Jewish laws. As more and more gentiles were converted the question arose of whether the new gentile converts should conform to the traditional Jewish law. For example, should gentile men be circumcised, and should gentiles follow the strict Jewish dietary laws? To settle this issue the apostles and others met in Jerusalem. Here

Peter reminded his audience that he had been chosen to take the Good News to the gentiles. (They would be familiar with his original visit to the Roman centurion, Cornelius; a visit precipitated by miraculous messages both to Peter and to Cornelius.) Paul and Barnabas told of their far-flung evangelization of the gentiles. After discussion, James took the lead to set out the decision of the participants: Gentiles did not need to follow Jewish law except on a very few points. This decision is expressed as being made "by the Holy Spirit and by ourselves..." (Acts 15:5–29). The implication is that the decision is not just a reasonable one based on the evidence, but that it is informed by the Holy Spirit. It is authoritative such that the Christian believer is bound to accept it.

Subsequent councils were called over the centuries, some more local and some more general. "Ecumenical" councils were those which included representatives from the whole Church. Leaders of most Christian denominations have accepted the decisions of at least the first seven of such ecumenical councils, which met before the Great Schism between Eastern and Western Christendom.[35] Catholics acknowledge the authority of twenty-one, the most recent being Vatican II in the twentieth century. For our purposes here – and central to Church teaching down the ages – are the First Council of Nicaea (325 CE) and The Council of Chalcedon (451 CE).[36] Nicaea explained how the Trinity is to be understood: God is three persons, and yet one nature or substance. That the Christian God is triune is not seen to conflict with the strict monotheism rooted in Judaism. Chalcedon confirmed the doctrine of the Incarnation: Jesus Christ is one person with two natures, a human nature and a divine nature as the Second Person of the Trinity. Christ is a single Person who is both fully God and fully human. (Though Augustine is writing before this council, his views on the Incarnation are in accord with it.) Clearly these are very difficult doctrines. Each seems to introduce a dilemma. How can something be both three persons, yet one, unified nature? And how can one person be both human and divine?

One way to "solve" the dilemmas is to abandon one side or the other. The reason these two critical councils were called to solidify Church teaching was that influential thinkers and churchmen had done exactly that. For example, some had interpreted the trinitarian hints from the Bible and earlier tradition as the unified God *appearing* in three different modes; as Father in the Old Testament, as Son in Jesus, and as Holy Spirit subsequently. But this approach denied that Father, Son, and Spirit were different beings in any way at all. Alternatively, other thinkers focused on the *threeness* of God. One influential view was Arianism; Father, Son, and Spirit are all divine, but there is a hierarchy in God such that the Father is the highest being, the Son somewhat lower, and the Spirit third.

A different insistence on the threeness argued that the three persons, though coequal, must be distinct individuals with a multiplicity akin to that of three angels or three human beings. (This "social trinitarianism" was revived in the eleventh century, and again in the nineteenth century, and is entertained by some contemporary philosophers and theologians.) The same sort of "solution" had been applied to the dilemma of the Incarnation. On the one hand, some denied the humanity of Christ. For example, Jesus merely *appeared* to be a human being, but was really just God presenting an illusion. Conversely, some denied the divinity of Jesus. Jesus was just a very special human being. Both of these approaches to the Incarnation, with a dazzling variety of permutations, gained steam because many intellectuals took a dim view of matter and found it gross that God might actually be joined to a human body.

The First Council of Nicaea and the Council of Chalcedon insisted that orthodoxy embrace the more difficult doctrines of the Trinity and the Incarnation. However, as is the way with Church Councils, they did not explain how to deal with the apparent dilemmas. Church Councils do not produce treatises on metaphysics. The philosopher or theologian accepting the authority of the councils may find that the job is to clarify difficult doctrines and defend them against attackers. That is how Augustine and Anselm and Aquinas view their work vis-à-vis the hard questions. AAA take it that the councils were guided by the Holy Spirit as they deliberated concerning the Trinity and the Incarnation, evaluating the traditional teachings and the Scriptural evidence passed down from the earliest Christians and assessing the philosophical and theological implications. AAA see that the conciliar conclusions are hard to understand, yet all insist that, even if one cannot understand them, one must accept them. But all agree that – at least for those members of the Church whose job is philosophy and theology – the attempt to understand must be made. And all conclude that it is possible to gain some vision – if dim and distant – of the triune nature of God and His saving work in Christ as expressed by the councils.

The Reasonableness of Faith

Acceptance of the claims that generate the hard questions are matters of faith. But is it stupid to commit to certain beliefs on faith? Augustine tells us in his *Confessions* – the story of his rejection of, and return to, Christianity – that one of the main reasons for his early rejection of Christianity was that it asked people to believe some things on faith. "Faith", as a general term in Augustine's understanding, does not mean an arbitrary commitment through brute will in the absence of evidence. In its most general sense it means belief based on the testimony of others. For example, the resurrection of Jesus, if it happened, is an historical fact, and could only be witnessed by people at the time. If the later Christian believes that Christ rose from the dead, his belief is based on the testimony of others. Early on Augustine held that believing something on faith did not rise to his high standards of epistemic virtue.

Eventually Augustine realized that most of what he believed, he believed on the testimony of others – beliefs about events he had not witnessed, places he had not gone, subjects he had not studied – and that one could not get on with life being skeptical about these things. His favorite example is the belief that your parents are your parents. You believe this only because you were told it. Augustine concluded that Christians were just being honest when they admitted that some important beliefs had to be accepted on faith.[37] It is true that believing some things on faith increases your risk of believing something false. And that is not a good thing. Is the safest epistemic move to withhold assent to any, or most, belief? That way you can avoid believing something false. But radical skepticism means failing to believe what is true. And that is a problem as well. Augustine's reevaluation of the reasonableness of accepting some things on faith formed one key aspect of his return to Christianity.

Anselm, having thoroughly embraced the teachings of Augustine, often repeats the value, indeed necessity, of believing the teachings of the Church on faith. But in several of his philosophical works, having made the point about faith, he will then go on to try to *prove* the doctrine in question through reason. Scholars debate whether he really intends to prove the doctrine through reason to someone who rejects it or, instead, is his goal to help explain and deepen the belief of someone who already accepts the doctrine on faith. In Anselm's case, this may be a false dichotomy. Anselm aims his arguments at believers and nonbelievers alike, hoping to strengthen the former's beliefs at the same time that he tries to persuade the latter to believe. But it is beyond doubt that he agrees with Augustine that it is reasonable to accept the teachings of the Church on faith.

In the thirteenth century when Aquinas was at work in Paris the issue of the distinction between faith and reason became crucial. The entry of the body of Aristotle's writing into Western Europe occasioned a great deal of exciting philosophy. But some intellectuals embraced Aristotle uncritically. To them "truth" meant what reason, that is "science", could prove, and "science" meant Aristotle.[38] But Aristotle says things that conflict with Christian belief. For example, Aristotle holds that the past is infinite, things have always been going on as they go on now, and God does not step into the world to perform miraculous, watershed events, after which human history takes a new direction. For a Christian (or a Jew or a Muslim) this Aristotelian conclusion conflicts with central tenets of their religious belief. Thus there was heated debate over how Aristotle should be treated. Aquinas, though in many ways an Aristotelian, does not swallow every claim made by the Philosopher (as Aristotle was called). And one aspect of Aquinas's caution toward Aristotle lies in his careful analysis of the limits of human reason. Reason can, for example, prove that God exists. But, says Aquinas, reason cannot prove that God is a Trinity. Aquinas holds that our knowledge begins with observation of the world around us. Given the extent to which God transcends creation it would be unreasonable to suppose that human cognition could fathom the depths of the divine. Nonetheless it is important for us to hold the correct beliefs about God. Hence God has graciously revealed the truths about Himself that it is important for us to accept on faith.[39]

It would be silly to believe everything everyone says. There are principles for when it is reasonable to commit to a particular claim. For one thing, one should consider the source. AAA hold that the evidence is that the founders of Christianity are trustworthy.[40] Scripture is trustworthy, and Scripture describes the establishment of the Church on which God bestows His Spirit. Hence the statements of the councils are produced by an impeccable source. Another consideration is how well a claim fits with other things one knows, or reasonably believes, to be true. Take faith in the Incarnation as an example. AAA agree that the existence of God can be proven philosophically. That God exists is not a claim one need accept on faith. But looking at human evil, it seems that something has gone badly amiss with humanity since the dawn of history. It seems plausible that an omnipotent, perfectly good God would do *something* to remedy humanity's miserable situation. Thus the testimony that Christ is God and the Risen Savior, though strange, fits well into the picture of a universe made good by God, but occupied by creatures who seem to be desperately in need of help. Anselm argues along these lines that he can *prove* that God *had to* become incarnate. Most philosophers and theologians, including Aquinas, think Anselm was too optimistic here. But even if he has not *proven* that the Incarnation was necessary, he has offered reasons to trust the testimony of the early Christians.

Once one commits to the belief that Jesus was God incarnate it becomes reasonable to assent to other core doctrines of Christianity in that they are expressed by Jesus as quoted in Scripture, or by those who knew Jesus, or in that they are decided upon by the Church Jesus founded and upon whom He breathed his Spirit. But, in discussing the approach of AAA, there is one more crucial point to make about faith in Christian doctrine. It is one emphasized by both Augustine and Anselm, and Aquinas sets it out clearly in his *Summa theologiae* in the first several questions in 2-2 (the Second Part of the Second Part): Believing in Christian doctrines on faith involves choice. Some beliefs you have acquired without any act of will. Their truth is so evident that you just accept them. You can't help but believe that 2 + 2 = 4 as soon as you see what it means. And (barring too much philosophy) you can't help but believe that there is an elephant there when you are looking at an elephant. And you may accept many beliefs automatically, on testimony, no choosing involved. Augustine's example of your belief that your parents are your parents would be such a case. Faith in Christian doctrines functions differently. Here faith is a virtue – one of the three theological virtues, faith, hope, and charity. It is a moral matter whether one possesses and nourishes these virtues, and so it is a matter, not just of thinking or believing, but of willing. Although it is reasonable to believe these doctrines, they do not appear to your mind as something you inevitably believe. You must decide to embrace them or not. Aquinas holds, and Augustine and Anselm agree, that the act of choice embracing Christian doctrines requires divine grace. Augustine makes this clear even as he is defending the general reasonableness and usefulness of embracing many beliefs on the testimony of others. Because of the miserable condition of fallen humanity, we need extra help from God to commit to the important doctrines. AAA and almost all Christians past and present have held that commitment to Christianity requires grace. What grace is, and how grace works, and to whom God gives grace, are among the hard questions dealt with in Chapter Four. So it may be reasonable to believe core doctrines of Christianity on faith, but nevertheless it is a matter of choice and requires grace.

Miracles

The Incarnation and the Resurrection of Jesus can be considered "miracles". But what is a miracle? We might describe all sorts of amazing things as miracles. A very bright comet might seem "miraculous", as might the conception of a child. But we are interested in a specific meaning of "miracle", the miracles associated with the hard questions of Christianity. Someone might argue that Christianity is obviously false because it incorporates events that lie outside of the laws of nature. Christianity believes in miracles, and miracles are "unscientific", therefore Christianity is opposed to science and hence false. AAA would take that stance to be philosophically naïve. God is the author of nature and is free to introduce events and entities that are not a part of the scientific picture of the universe. A miracle is an event that does not follow the usual course of nature and is produced by God to make a point. The evidence is that God very much likes secondary causation, the system of cause and effect that He produces in our universe, and so miracles will be few and far between. But there is nothing in the relationship of divine primary causation causing scientific secondary causation that would preclude God's doing something unusual.

It is sometimes said that a miracle is "against" the course of nature. If that means that God destroys some good thing or undermines secondary causation, then AAA do not explain miracles that way. Indeed, Augustine has been accused, by some modern commentators, of taking too "naturalistic" an approach to miracles. By and large, he is concerned to describe miracles in a way that portrays God working with secondary causes, but just in an unusual way. For example, in our experience "all men are mortal", but Augustine holds that death is the wages of sin. It is not a constitutive element of human *nature*, only a sad necessity of fallen humanity. That Jesus is resurrected is part of the reconstruction of the human race, wherein God restores the soul to the dead body.[41] (More on resurrection in Chapter Six.) When God (through Moses) changes the stick into a snake, or when Jesus changes the water into wine, the process of transforming this material thing into some other material thing is one that nature does all the time, only more slowly. Moreover, says Augustine, it is unreasonable for us to believe that we understand all of the hidden properties in things. When God created all that would unfold over the course of time He did so through "seminal reasons" – "seeds" that contained the potencies that things would eventually exhibit. God, being eternal and omniscient, always knew what miracles He intended to accomplish and so, says Augustine, perhaps he included the potencies for the unusual events in those seminal reasons. And then, when the time is right, the potencies unfolded.[42] And God is keeping everything in being from moment to moment *ex nihilo*, so if He adds some new entity to the physical universe, that does not entail the destruction of the nature of things already here. Jesus's conception in a virgin is certainly miraculous, but it is not *against* nature.

Anselm has little to say about the miraculous. He explains that events may happen due to God's will alone, or due to God's will and the natural activity of a created cause (secondary causation), or due to the will of a created agent. The first sort of event, like Christ's conception in the Virgin, is a miracle. It is an event not governed by the laws of nature or by created agency. But the miracle does not "harm" these other causal systems when it seems to oppose them. Everything that exists exists by the will of God and sometimes God acts without secondary causation.[43] Other miraculous conceptions, such as John the Baptist's, are even more in keeping with the natural course of things. John was conceived after his

mother, Elizabeth, was past the age of childbearing. God *repairs* a biological system which had ceased functioning due to age, but the weakness
and disability are not a product of human nature *per se* but inhere in fallen
humanity due to original sin.[44] So, like Augustine, Anselm embraces the
miraculous, but holds that in performing miracles God in no way subverts
or destroys natural processes.

Aquinas is more willing to say that God may act *contrary* to nature. He
writes, "A miracle is *contrary* to nature, when nature retains a disposition
contrary to the effect produced by God: for instance when he prevented
the three children in the furnace from being hurt, while the fire retained
the power to burn".[45] But even here the claim is not that God destroys the
fire or somehow negates its nature. God kept the fire from burning the
three young men, though it remained fire, with the causal power natural
to fire. When God produces an unusual effect, not through secondary
causation, in order to impress some point on those who observe or learn
about it, that is a miracle. But miracles happen alongside the course of
nature. They are not *against* nature if that means destructive of natural
things and processes. Nor would AAA see belief in miracles as opposed
to science. The claim is that the entities and principles of the various
sciences do not exhaust reality. God, the author of all reality other than
Himself, may choose to step in and do something unusual. (Aquinas does
caution that fully natural events might look like miracles if the causes are
hidden.[46])

What role do miracles play in the world view of AAA? The Incarnation
and Resurrection of Jesus are defining events of Christianity. AAA do not
take them to prove the existence of God. Philosophical arguments show
that God exists. If you were convinced of atheism, you would likely not
credit the reports of such miracles. If, on the other hand, you are convinced that God exists and is omnipotent and good and personal, you
might be more open minded about belief in these miracles. (Jesus was
not born among atheists, after all, but among people who were already
committed to belief in a God Who takes an interest in us.) And if you
had a deep sense of your own weakness and failings (more on original
sin in Chapter Two), the thought that God might take drastic action for
the salvation of humankind would seem plausible. And if you found the
testimony credible – the witnesses tend to agree, seem to be generally
truthful, seem to believe what they are reporting, would not benefit by
lying, etc. – you might accept these miracles of the Christian faith (assuming you have been helped along by divine grace). The evidence of these
miracles cannot be invoked to prove the existence of God. That would be
begging the question, since you would be unlikely to accept the miracles
unless you already believed in God. But this evidence might encourage

you to adopt Christian theism over other versions of monotheism.[47] A stumbling block to accepting Christianity is that it does involve some difficult doctrines. The hope of this book is to suggest how AAA address the hard questions and mitigate the apparent problems.

Note on Citations

Different primary texts cited in this book are arranged differently. I have tried to cite to make it easy for the reader – especially one who is new to looking at late classical and medieval texts – to access the text in question. When texts are divided into several books, I have spelled out "Book". Then I have given the chapter number and, if I am focusing on a specific section within a chapter, I have given that number as well. "*On the Trinity* Book 4.13.2" refers to the fourth book of Augustine's *On the Trinity*, Chapter 13, section 2. Citations covering consecutive chapters or sections use a hyphen. "*On the Trinity* Book 4.13.2-5" refers to sections 2 through 5. If I am referring to several nonconsecutive chapters or sections in the same text I use "and". "*On the Trinity* Book 4.13.2 and 5" refers to two separate sections in Chapter 13, sections 2 and 5. References to Aquinas's *Summa contra gentiles* (SCG) follow this pattern. If a text is not divided into books, as most of Anselm's are not, the citation is just the name of the work and the chapter. For example, "*Proslogion* 2" refers to Chapter Two of Anselm's *Proslogion*.

The standard way to cite Aquinas's *Summa theologiae* (ST) can seem tricky, but I follow it because it actually makes it easier for the reader to navigate the work. ST is divided into three main parts. "ST 1" refers to Part One. But the second part is divided into two parts, and the traditional way to reference them is as the First Part of the Second Part (ST 1-2) and the Second Part of the Second Part (ST 2-2). Part Three has a Supplement that I have cited as ST 3 Supp. Each part of ST is divided into questions, cited as "Q.". "ST 1 Q. 5" refers to Question 5 in Part 1 of ST. Each question is subdivided into articles, cited as "art.". "ST 1 Q. 5 art. 2" refers to Article 2 under Question 5 in ST 1. Each article is divided further, since Aquinas begins each article with the objections to the view he is going to defend. "ST 1 Q. 5 art. 2 obj. 3" refers to the third objection that Aquinas raises against his own position at the beginning of the second article in Question 5 of ST 1. At the end of each article Aquinas responds to each objection in turn. "ST 1 Q. 5 art. 2 ad 3" refers to the response to Objection 3. "Ad" is the Latin for "to". If the article is listed, but not followed by "obj." or "ad", that means that the citation is to the main body of the article where Aquinas is expressing and explaining his own position. This can seem complex, but once you get into it, the organization makes it easy to find specific topics, and the objections and responses ensure that all the pros and cons of which Aquinas is aware get on the table.

Outline of the Book

Chapter One: The Trinity

Chapter One addresses how Augustine, Anselm, and Aquinas understand the doctrine of the divine Trinity; the claim that God is three persons, yet one, unified nature. After discussing what "person" might mean, the chapter explains AAA's view that it is the relationships between the persons that distinguishes them. This explanation is developed through Augustine's analogy for the Trinity, the thinking human mind. The mind is one thing, yet thinking requires a dynamic interrelationship between memory, understanding, and will. Anselm's proof for the Trinity drawn from Augustine's analogy is then outlined. The chapter concludes with a look at Aquinas's responses to a number of problems raised with this way of thinking about the Trinity.

Chapter Two: Original Sin

Chapter Two explores AAA's understanding of the doctrine of original sin. Original sin is a disorder or infection affecting all of humanity such that we all tend toward doing evil. It stems from the first sin of the first people, Adam and Eve. This introduces two related problems: Why does God permit evil choices? And what sort of free will do human beings have? AAA agree that God permits evil choices because of the value of free will and in order to bring good out of them. But, regarding the nature of free will, Augustine and Aquinas are compatibilists while Anselm is a libertarian. Thus they propose different causal explanations for the Fall of Adam and Eve. The transmission of original sin introduces a new problem. Augustine sees original sin as a stain, while Anselm sees it as an absence. Aquinas seems to adopt both approaches and also to emphasize the damage original sin does to human nature.

Chapter Three: The Incarnation

Chapter Three addresses two questions regarding the Incarnation, that is God the Son assuming a human nature as Jesus Christ. The first is: Couldn't He have saved humanity simply by willing that humanity be saved? AAA argue, for a number of reasons, that the Incarnation was the most effective way to achieve the salvation of humanity. Anselm goes so far as to claim to prove that the Incarnation was necessary. The second question is: How can a single person be both divine and human? The properties associated with divinity seem opposed to those associated with humanity. For example, God is omniscient, human knowledge is limited. God is omnipotent, human abilities are limited. AAA adopt the "qua" move: Jesus Christ has divine properties qua God and human properties qua human. This is not easy to imagine, but it is coherent.

Chapter Four: Grace

Chapter Four discusses how AAA assess the need for divine grace to reach heaven. In Augustine's day a churchman named Pelagius and his followers had proposed that grace was not necessary; the human being could freely choose to be good enough to merit heaven. Or, if grace was necessary, one could freely be good enough to deserve it. Augustine criticizes these claims on two counts. First, divine omnipotence is limited if God "owes" it to the created agent to save him. Second, if human beings can save themselves, Christ's Incarnation, passion, and resurrection were pointless. AAA agree that grace is necessary and unmerited. Then does free will play any role at all in the salvation of the individual? In reconciling grace and free will Anselm gives free will a more decisive role than do Augustine and Aquinas. Further questions concerning grace include: Why does God give grace to some and not to others? And, Can you know if you have received the grace that will allow you to persevere on the heaven-bound path to the end of your life?

Chapter Five: Divine Foreknowledge and Human Free Will

Chapter Five deals with a perennial question in the philosophy of religion: How can divine foreknowledge be reconciled with human freedom? That is, if God knows today what you will choose tomorrow, you necessarily choose as God foreknows. But if your choice happens necessarily, then you are not free. AAA insist that God knows future events and that human beings have free will. Augustine points out that the "necessity" involved in foreknowledge is not the "necessity" that conflicts with free will. Boethius (480–524 CE) adds that God "sees" all events from His perspective in eternity. But Boethius concludes that God foreknows all events because He is going to cause them. Anselm, given his libertarian analysis of free will, holds that God knows future free choices because they are immediately present to His eternity. This motivates an "isotemporal" (four-dimensional, eternalist) view of time on which all times exist equally, and past, present, and future are subjective. Aquinas may or may not be an isotemporalist. As a compatibilist he can embrace Boethius's claim that God knows future events because He intends to cause them.

Chapter Six: The Afterlife

Chapter Six deals with Augustine and Aquinas on the soul and body and heaven and hell. (Anselm is not featured until the section on hell, since he did not write extensively on the soul or the afterlife.) After a quick proof of heaven, the topic is the nature of the human person, a unity of soul and body together. Augustine and Aquinas both offer proofs for the incorporeal nature of the soul and its immortality. A more challenging issue is the resurrection of the body. Augustine, especially, works to defend this doctrine against Platonists who find it absurd. What will the afterlife be like for those in heaven? They will enjoy eternal happiness beholding God. What about hell? Augustine and Aquinas are compatibilists, meaning that God could have drawn everyone into heaven without damaging their free will. He did not do so because the damned serve various purposes that are likely to strike the modern reader as uncharitable. Anselm's libertarianism allows for a more satisfactory explanation for why hell is not empty: God respects our free agency to such an extent that He allows us to choose hell.

Chapter Seven: Christian Exclusivity

Chapter Seven discusses Christianity as an exclusive religion. One can be saved only through faith in Jesus Christ, but AAA hold that anyone might receive grace and salvation. Baptism is necessary but, in practice, is available to everyone. Nor is everyone who professes Christianity assured of salvation. How should non-Christians be treated? The focus is on Augustine as the foundation for Anselm and Aquinas. Islam is mentioned only briefly since it arose after Augustine's death. Augustine confronted several heresies. His main tool is argument, but he concludes that the state may use force against heresy in the interests of social order and Church unity. Aquinas agrees. In the context of their times their positions are moderate. What of the Jews? They are not heretics, since a heretic must claim to be a Christian. Augustine defends the Jews, insisting, against opponents, that Jesus and His disciples were Jews who followed the Jewish law. The Jews are protected by God, and it is important that their community survive, since, through their holy books they serve as witnesses to the antiquity of the divine plan for humanity's salvation through Christ.

Notes

1 Neoplatonism begins with the late classical project, exemplified mainly by Plotinus, of systematizing Plato's thought and reconciling it with that of Aristotle. Augustine records how helpful he found the "books of the Platonists", though he also notes that they fall dismally short of Christian revelation. See his *Confessions* Book 7.9-21.

2 None of Aquinas's famous "Five Ways" to prove the existence of God depends upon the assumption of a temporal beginning to the created universe, nor does any of them *conclude* to a temporal beginning. The Five Ways are found in the *Summa theologiae* (ST 1 Q. 2 art. 3). A temporal beginning to the universe cannot be proven by reason but must be accepted on faith (ST 1 Q. 46 art. 2). In doing philosophy one must allow the possibility that the past is infinite.

3 Anselm explains that what is necessary and what is possible depend on the will of God. But, since God is eternal and immutable, and it is good that logic be what it is, there is no question of logic changing (*Cur deus homo (Why God Became Man)* Book 2.17).

4 Aquinas, ST 1-2 (First Part of the Second Part) Q. 94.

5 See also, Augustine, *On the Literal Meaning of Genesis* Book 3.16.

6 See Augustine's *Confessions* Book 7.12.

7 See Anselm's *Cur deus homo* Book 2.5, 10, and 17.

8 See Aquinas's *Summa contra gentiles* (SCG) Book 1.81.

9 Aquinas, ST 1 Q. 14.

10 Aquinas, ST 1 Q. 3. The simplicity of God is the first divine attribute that Aquinas discusses immediately after proving the existence of God in the *Summa theologiae*.

11 Anselm, *Proslogion* 18.

12 That God is pure act, with no potentiality, is the conclusion of the first of Aquinas's Five Ways (ST 1 Q. 2 art. 3). In the discussion of divine simplicity Aquinas argues that God's very essence is His act of being (ST 1 Q. 3 art. 4). Augustine and Anselm, too, take God to be an act (Anselm, *Monologion* 4).

13 Aquinas, ST 1 Q. 9.

14 For divine immutability see Aquinas, ST 1 Q. 14 art. 15 and Q. 19 art. 7. That God is not really related to creatures see ST 1 Q. 28 arts. 1 ad 3.

15 Anselm *On the Harmony of God's Foreknowledge, Predestination, and Grace with Free Choice* (I will call this work *De concordia*, which means "On the Harmony...") Book 1.5.

16 Aquinas, ST 1 Q. 26.

17 SCG Book 3. 69.12–20.

18 Augustine, *On the Literal Meaning of Genesis* Book 4.16. He repeats Plato's *Timaeus* that God, being "without envy", must bring every good thing into existence.

19 On animals eating one another see Augustine, *On the Literal Meaning of Genesis* Book 3.16.

20 Aquinas, ST 1 Q. 22 art. 2.

21 See also, Augustine, *On the Teacher* 12.

22 For "just" see *On Truth* 12 and for "free" see *On Free Choice* 1.

23 ST 1 Q. 85 art. 1.

24 ST 1 Q. 13 arts. 2–5.

25 ST 1 Q. 13 art. 6.

26 ST 1 Q. 2 art. 3.

27 Maimonides, the great medieval Jewish philosopher (1138–1204 CE), offers a different negative way in which positive terms should be understood as the

negation of their opposite. God is good and wise means He is not bad or stupid, but this does not tell us anything about how God is in Himself. Aquinas rejects this (ST 1 Q. 13 art. 2).

28 Anselm, *Proslogion* 14. A proponent of this sort of *via negativa* is Pseudo-Dionysius, whom Aquinas quotes often (ST 1 Q. 12 art. 1 Obj. 3 and reply). Sometimes Aquinas does speak as if he subscribes to a more "pure" negation (SCG Book 1.14).

29 Augustine, *On the Trinity* Book 15.27; Anselm, *Monologion* 54, *On the Incarnation of the Word* 1; Aquinas, SCG Book 4.1.10.

30 Augustine, *On the Literal Meaning of Genesis* Book 1.10.

31 Augustine, *On the Literal Meaning of Genesis* Book 6.10–11.

32 Book 1.19.

33 Augustine, *On Christian Doctrine*. See also *On the Literal Meaning of Genesis* Book 1.1 and 20–21.

34 AAA take the ultimate author of the Bible to be God, so they might hold that the interpretive principles set out above are more fundamental than the historical approach favored by many contemporary biblical scholars.

35 Sometimes 1054 is given as the decisive date of the Great Schism, but there had been a long history of growing division for centuries before that year. Moreover, efforts at reproachment were made after 1054 indicating that East and West did not see reunification as a lost cause. And perhaps history will yet prove the optimists right.

36 Norman P. Tanner, *Decrees of the Ecumenical Councils* Two-Volume Set (Georgetown University Press, 1990).

37 *Confessions* Book 6.5.

38 These were the so-called "Latin Averroists", named after the great commentator on Aristotle, Averroes (Ibn Rushd) whose work entered Western Europe along with Aristotle's.

39 ST 1 Q. 1, art. 1.

40 The early Church debated over which texts should be considered authoritative and appealed to several different principles to make the determination. (Augustine mentions some in *On Christian Doctrine* Book 2.8.12.)

41 *City of God* Book 13.1.

42 *On the Literal Meaning of Genesis* Book 6.13–14. The snake and the wine are also mentioned in Augustine's *On the Trinity* Book 3. 5.

43 *On the Virgin Conception and Original Sin* 11.

44 *On the Virgin Conception and Original Sin* 16.

45 *On Power* Q. 6 art. 2 ad 3. See also ST 1 Q. 105 arts. 6–8, SCG Book 3.100–102.

46 *On Power* Q. 6 art. 2.

47 Augustine holds that many miracles were performed to win people over to Christian belief. He reports that miracles continue to happen and offers a list of miracles he has witnessed himself or heard about from credible sources (*City of God* Book 22.8).

1

THE TRINITY

Introduction

The Council of Nicaea in 325 stated that God is three "persons", Father, Son, and Holy Spirit. The three persons have one nature. They are one "substance", one individual being, and hence only one God. At first glance this looks to be contradictory. Something that is one cannot be three, can it? The math just does not add up. In the present chapter, I sketch how Augustine, Anselm, and Aquinas (AAA) approach the difficult question of the Trinity. The goal is to show that it is possible to gain a distant cognitive glimpse of the triune God. This glimpse supports the claim that the doctrine of the Trinity is not contradictory, that is, it does not say that God is both one and three *in the same way at the same time*. After some introductory remarks, we will look at AAA's claim that it is their relationships to one another that distinguish the three persons, then we will consider Augustine's analogy of the human mind to help "glimpse" the Trinity. A quick discussion of Anselm's "proof" that God is a Trinity follows, and then a brief look at Aquinas's approach.

I will not be presenting a developed historical case for the opinions of AAA, but, in reviewing some basic ideas, I hope to provide enough citations to their work to steer the reader who would like more information toward some of the relevant primary texts. Nor will I be attempting to canvas the relevant contemporary literature.[1] That would require an expedition deep into the current metaphysical weeds, and a trip of that nature lies outside the scope of the present introductory work. And finally, I will not be discussing scriptural support for the doctrine of the Trinity. Again, that would be too extensive a task. The reader interested in biblical sources for the doctrine of the Trinity would do well to look at Augustine's very long book, *On the Trinity*, which begins with an exhaustive review of what he takes to be references to the Trinity in both the New and Old Testaments.[2]

DOI: 10.4324/9781003202080-2

Before beginning our attempt to glimpse the Trinity, it is important to make several introductory points. The first will be relevant to all the chapters of this book: It is very often the case that something looks simple until you really start to think about it. The more exact and clear you try to become in the analysis of any issue, the more difficult, complex, puzzling, and sometimes paradoxical it can get. Augustine makes this point about the nature of time in Book 11 of his *Confessions*. As long as no one asks him to explain what time is, he has a grasp on it. Once the question is put to him, he finds that the nature of time is deeply elusive. This is the standard progression for considering pretty much any philosophical issue you choose; it looks easy and obvious until you try to think carefully, but then it gets hard and weird almost immediately. I think most philosophers would agree with me here. Take a quick look into the *Stanford Encyclopedia of Philosophy* on topics that are relevant to the Trinity.[3] You could check out the general philosophical area, "mereology", which is the study of the relationship between parts and wholes. What you would discover is that even the issue of what the term "part" *means* is actively debated, while the metaphysical questions of what a part *is* and (perhaps a somewhat different question) what sorts of things are parts, are open to numerous perplexing answers each with its advantages and disadvantages. If "parts" are hard to understand, what about "wholes"? Look up "objects" and "ordinary objects". The fact that there are two separate entries signals at the outset that things are likely to get pretty strange pretty fast. And sure enough, what the term "object" means, and what counts as an object, turn out to be amazingly hard questions to which philosophers have given all sorts of answers, many of which, at least prima facie, seem bizarre. Maybe any combination of things should be considered an object. So the Milky Way and Elon Musk and your left shoe, taken together, constitute an object. Maybe only living organisms have the necessary unity to be considered objects. Maybe there just are no objects to speak of. And on and on. And often even appreciating the force of the argument leading to the bizarre conclusion does not mitigate the bizarreness. The point is this: We should not dismiss the difficult claims of Christianity as false because they are hard to understand and seem to lead to puzzles and paradoxes. *Anything and everything*, when carefully considered, is hard to understand and seems to lead to puzzles and paradoxes. Reality is strange, and if you don't think so you're not paying attention.[4]

A second introductory point is especially relevant to the doctrine of the Trinity, though it is important for other doctrines as well: God is very unlike creatures. This might seem obvious, and yet philosophers, past and present, sometimes fail to remember it. For example, one sometimes finds contemporary philosophers appealing to analyses of the relationship of parts to wholes that are drawn from material objects and then trying to apply those analyses to the Trinity. They adopt a mereological theory applicable to "some being X", and then suppose that "X" could be God or "X" could be your cat or your phone. Augustine, in his *On the Trinity*, laid the groundwork for subsequent discussion of the Trinity in the Western world, and he never tires of insisting that we must resist the temptation to think of the divine in creaturely – especially material – terms. We suffer from this temptation because sensible things are familiar to us, so it is difficult to avoid assuming that the same "rules" that apply to the physical world around us must apply to God. For example, if you have a corporeal thing, and then you add another similar corporeal thing to it, and then another, the three together will likely be more than the first one alone. But this principle of addition does not apply to the three persons of the Trinity. You don't get more God by adding the Son to the Father, the Holy Spirit to the Son, etc., God is just different from created things.[5]

A final point about terminology is in order. The Trinity is said to be one God, one nature, but three persons. How should we understand the term "persons"? We could insist that the term must be used as we ordinarily use it today. Roughly, a "person" is a discrete individual who is, or has the potential to be, a rational agent.[6] If it is supposed that Father, Son, and Holy Spirit are each discrete individuals, each with His own private intellect and will, then the unity required for the one God is abandoned. Anselm argued against this "tritheist" position when it was suggested by a monk named Roscelin in the eleventh century. More recently, it has been revived under the label "social trinitarianism". Augustine attempts to forestall the rejection of divine unity by holding that we should not understand the term "person" in a way that would dissolve God's oneness. Yes, there is a certain threeness in God. Father, Son, and Holy Spirit are distinct. Yet they are not discrete individuals the way three human beings or three angels would be. There is no word that captures just what Father, Son, and Holy Spirit are three of. "Persons" is a sort of placeholder, since some word has to be used, and it would not do to say they are three "somethings". But "person" here is not used as it would be when talking about three human individuals.[7]

Anselm repeats the concern over the term "person", granting, as did Augustine, that some word has to be used, and "person" is about the best we can do.[8] At first glance, Aquinas might seem to depart from Augustine and Anselm over "person". He defends the common medieval understanding of "person" as appropriately applied to both human and divine persons. Aquinas repeats the standard definition derived from Boethius (480–524 CE). A person is "… an individual substance of a rational nature". But Aquinas does go on to point out that "person" must be used

somewhat differently of God and a created person.[9] Moreover, well before he began discussing the Trinity Aquinas had proposed his doctrine of
analogy (discussed in the "Introduction") to explain how our words and
concepts apply to God: Our words and concepts have a different, but related meaning. They are used "equivocally", but not *purely* equivocally.[10]
Augustine and Anselm may feel more of a need to emphasize the worry
over the use of the term "person" since, for many divine attributes – God
is good, God is wise, etc. – they allow that there is an underlying sameness
("univocity") when those terms are used of God and creatures.[11] Aquinas,
having already insisted that our words are used equivocally of creatures
and of God, may consider it sufficient, in discussing the Trinity, to remind
the reader that "person" is used differently of God and created persons.
Thus AAA all warn us that we should not be led astray by the term "person" into thinking there must be three, separate individuals in the Trinity,
each with His own intellect and will.

Relations between the Three Divine Persons

God is one, simple being. He is one act of omnipotence, omniscience,
perfect goodness, etc.[12] As Anselm points out to Roscelin, if one posited
three really discrete divine beings, none of them would be "that than
which nothing greater can be conceived". For example, take the attribute
of omnipotence. If there were three divinities, each of the three – since
none could be subservient to another – would be confronted by beings
over which its power does not extend.[13] But a being whose power is thus
limited is not God. So it is not the case that in God the operations of
divinity are somehow divided between the three persons. No, each is omnipotent, omniscient, perfectly good, etc., with the same power, knowledge, goodness, etc., of the other two. How, then, are Father, Son, and
Holy Spirit distinct? AAA are in rough agreement that the three persons
of the Trinity are distinguished through their relationships to one another. First, we will look at their explanation of this difficult view. This
may leave the reader feeling dissatisfied. One may credit AAA with offering an analysis that does indeed describe the triune God in such a way that
both the oneness and the threeness are respected and yet feel that one
does not have any "grasp" on what the Trinity is like. A perfectly respect-
able response to that uncomfortable feeling is that God is God, and one
should not expect to grasp the divine. But we may be able to do a little
better than that. Augustine offers an analogy of the Trinity drawn from
the closest reflection of God that we know, the human mind. It is just an
analogy, but it may go some distance toward allowing us, not to grasp the
Trinity, but at least to glimpse it.

What distinguishes the three persons within the Trinity is their eternal and immutable relations to one another.[14] It is important to remember that God is an act, and the internal relations that distinguish the persons are relations involving action. The Father "begets" the Son. The Son comes from the Father, but in a way that is nothing like *creation*. In creating, God chooses to make things that are, at best, barely existing, dim reflections of Himself. The Son comes from the Father by necessity, not by the Father's choosing. God is a necessary being. He could not possibly fail to exist and to be exactly what He is. Thus the internal relationships within the Trinity could not fail to exist and to be exactly what they are. The Son is the Father's "Word" in that He is the Father's self-expression.[15] In "speaking" Himself, the Father also makes whatever is created. Hence the Nicene Creed says of the Son that it is "through Him that all things are made". Although He "comes from" the Father, the Son is in no way inferior to, or lesser than, the Father.[16] On the contrary, the Son is "consubstantial" with the Father, that is, He is of the same being, equally God. How, then, are Father and Son distinct? The Father is the one who begets, but is not begotten, whereas the Son is the one who is begotten, but does not beget. The Holy Spirit "proceeds" from the Father and the Son.[17] Procession is a different process than being begotten, and the Holy Spirit is often described as the "Love" between the Father and the Son. As Love, the procession of the Holy Spirit can be seen as a "gifting" or a "sending forth". In the New Testament, we find many images of this procession. When John baptizes Jesus the Spirit descends upon Him like a dove. Jesus gives the Spirit to His disciples by breathing upon them. After Jesus's ascension into Heaven, at Pentecost, the followers of Jesus receive the Spirit as a great wind which divides into tongues of flame. The Holy Spirit is equally God and is distinguished from the Father and the Son by the relationship of being the one who proceeds from both.

The thought that the persons of the Trinity are distinguished by their relations to one another is puzzling. In creatures, as AAA explain, a relationship is what they would have called an "accidental" property, that is, roughly, a property belonging to a thing that is not essential for the thing to be what it is.[18] Hair color would be an accidental property of a human being. You are still human, no matter what color your hair is. You could dye your hair and be the same human being you were. Indeed you could lose all your hair and still be a human being and the same human being. The human analogs of the relationships within the Trinity are not constitutive of the nature of a human being – they are not essential properties – and they do not fundamentally distinguish one human being from another. Take fatherhood and sonship (AAA usually treat the Holy Spirit after making the point concerning Father and Son.) One might be a human being without being either a father or a son. Human beings can be fathers or sons, and the same person could be both a father and a son. Someone who was not a father could become a father without any fundamental change in who or what he is. A male human being is inevitably someone's son, but we might say that he could become someone else's son by adoption, while still remaining the same human being. With human beings the relationships of fatherhood and sonship are accidental properties.

God, as AAA insist, is very different from creatures. He does not have any accidental properties. The relationships that distinguish the persons in the triune God are necessary just as God, considered in His unified substance, is a necessary being. His very nature is to exist and to be what He is. Moreover, the relationships are eternal and immutable. In God Fatherhood, Sonship, and the Love between Father and Son, though they are relationships, have a unique divine status unlike that of the human relationships. God is one, dynamic act constituted internally by three dynamic relationships which distinguish the three persons. This does not seem to be logically contradictory. It is not that God is both A and not A in the same way at the same time. He is both one and three, but He is one in a different way from the way in which He is three.

Augustine's Analogy of the Mind

If the reader feels that he has not yet achieved the hoped-for "glimpse" of the Trinity, Augustine may be able to help. Augustine proposes an analogy – really a series of analogies – to help us come closer to glimpsing the Trinity. It is drawn from the human mind. Augustine takes the mind to be the thinking part of your nonphysical soul.[19] And he assumes that your mind is unified in that you are one thinking thing. Augustine believes that the body is an essential part of the individual human being, but it is the reasoning aspect of the soul that best reflects God. All created things reflect the divine more or less, but human beings are especially made in the image of God. We are images of God in that we have rational intellects and are free agents. So Augustine asks us to consider the human mind as it is thinking of something. Thinking is an action, and this makes the analogy apt since, as has already been mentioned, God is an act. In *On the Trinity*, Augustine discusses a series of analogies, ordered from least like, to most like, the Trinity. (He concludes the work by reviewing how even the closest analogy is very, very distant.) The least similar involves immediate perception of physical objects, and a discussion of Augustine's (very interesting, but somewhat complex) views on perception would lead us too far afield. For our purposes we can look at two of the analogies, the mind thinking of something it knows and the mind thinking of itself. A lot of time has passed since Augustine's day, and a lot of progress has been made in human psychology. Nevertheless his analysis stands up to introspection, and that is what is needed to appreciate his analogies.

So, first, take as an example you thinking about something that is not present to your perception but that you recognize – say, an ostrich.[20] In order to think about the ostrich, you must first access your memory. As Augustine points out, memory is a rather amazing thing. It is a vast storehouse of ideas and abilities, and it is there, doing its job, whether or not we are aware of it. And there is something mysterious about memory. It is a dark storehouse in that we cannot shine a cognitive light on "the memory" itself. We take a flashlight (not Augustine's imagery) and search out the particular item we are looking for. Weirdly, before we even remember, we must have some awareness of what we are looking for, since we know it when we find it. When we find what we are searching for we bring it out into cognitive awareness. As you remember, you are actively thinking about the ostrich. Your presently thinking the ostrich is one, unified action. But notice, says Augustine, how your one act of thinking involves three elements that can be seen to reflect the three persons of the Trinity. Memory is like the Father in that it brings forth something – your thinking of the ostrich – out of itself, which is of the same nature as itself. Your holding the ostrich in memory and then bringing it forth into your active thinking of the ostrich are aspects of one action. Your activity of understanding the ostrich, then, is like the Son. It is brought forth but shares the nature of its source. A third element is necessary for you to be thinking of the ostrich, and that is your will or desire. Will operates in two ways. Before the subject of ostriches came up, you were not thinking of an ostrich. Then you engaged in the process of looking in memory for the concept and brought it forth to present understanding. It requires a sort of "motion" of your will, or desire, to initiate that process connecting memory to thinking. Moreover, Augustine holds that that feeling of having remembered what you were trying to remember is a feeling of having a desire satisfied. He views love as a form of will or desire. So the will involved in your thinking of an ostrich is like the Holy Spirit Who is the Love connecting Father and Son and proceeding from both. With this discussion in mind, contemplate the act of thinking something. You have only one mind, and it is engaged in one mental activity, and yet we can discern three interrelated aspects or elements in that act.

The analogy of thinking something you recognize, like an ostrich, does not quite rise to being an image of God, according to Augustine. But change the example a little. Contemplate your mind thinking of itself. The three elements are at work, but the thinking is even more unified than when you were thinking of the ostrich. Your mind is a single being.[21]

When your mind thinks itself it remembers, understands, and wills (or loves) itself in one mental activity. And this, says Augustine, is a true image of God.[22] At least it allows us to glimpse how something which is unified can be a single dynamic act of three elements distinguished by their relations to one another. The mind is an even closer image of God when it remembers, understands, and loves Him, but this brings us almost to the realm of mystical vision.[23]

Having proposed this final analogy, Augustine, in the last book of *On the Trinity* lists a variety of disanalogies between the human mind and God. The human being is both soul and body, and it is difficult, as Augustine repeats, for the human being not to envision things in physical terms. Human beings are temporal, and so our thought processes move sequentially. We find it difficult, or impossible, to hold all of a thought before our minds at once.[24] Crucially, we are not simple beings even in our mental lives. The mind and its thinking are distinct. As Augustine says, it is appropriate to say that "I" am the one doing the remembering, the understanding, and the loving. But then "I" am not identical to these three. Rather, they "belong" to me.[25] And the three can differ in quantity from person to person. One person may have a better memory than another. The three can exist unequally even in one and the same person so that he may, for example, have an excellent memory but be lacking in love.[26] So, according to Augustine even the best image of the divine to which we have access is only a distant reflection. Still, it may give us a glimpse of the Trinity.

Anselm's Proof of the Trinity

Anselm takes Augustine as his guide in things philosophical and theological. And yet he differs from his master both in style and in content. Anselm's philosophical writing is less meditative and more analytic than Augustine's. His basic approach, and even his conclusions, are often different. His most extensive work on the Trinity is in his *Monologion*. In the Preface he explains that his brother Benedictine monks had asked him to set out some of his views on the divine essence, but he should expound them through necessary reasons and setting aside Scripture. He defends himself against the charge of introducing "novelties" – an undertaking frowned upon in the eleventh century – by suggesting that the critic should review Augustine's work on the Trinity. And it is true that, in one sense, the discussion of the Trinity in the *Monologion* follows Augustine's analysis closely. But Augustine was aiming at producing a useful analogy. Anselm, at least arguably, intends to *prove* that the divine must be a Trinity. Scholars debate about whether this can really be Anselm's intention. Aquinas, who is taken to be the paradigm philosopher in some circles, said that such a thing couldn't be done and that making the attempt causes more harm than good.[27] One reason many scholars immediately reject the thought that Anselm may hope to prove the Trinity is that they do not want to see him at odds with Aquinas. But Aquinas holds that our natural knowledge starts with experience of the physical world, and we know God only as the cause of the creation we observe around us.[28] Since it is the triune, but unified, God that creates, rather than any individual person of the Trinity, we cannot prove the Trinity by arguing from the created effect back to the divine cause. Augustine, and Anselm following him, embraced a different epistemology. As discussed in the Introduction, both held that much of our knowledge depends upon the direct action of God illumining our minds. God "shines" the truth into us. Thus the argument Aquinas makes against trying to prove the Trinity does not hold for Anselm. I take it that Anselm does hope to prove the Trinity, but on a very qualified understanding of what a "proof" might be. Anselm does believe in the Trinity as a matter of faith, and he thinks it is right for others to do the same. But he may also hold that the Trinity can be proven through reason. Anselm's arguments in his various works are often aimed at two goals, persuading the nonbeliever but also helping the believer to understand what he has already accepted on faith.[29] The possibility of a proof does not conflict with belief on faith and, even if the proof fails, that should not undermine belief.

One could take "proof" in a very strong sense. That is, one could suppose that a proof required, not only a correct (valid) logical form but also premises that any properly trained, rational person would recognize as true. In that case a genuine *proof* would be sound, the conclusion would follow as a matter of necessity, and any thoughtful person would have to agree with it. If that is what we mean by "proof" then Aquinas's critique of the attempt to prove that God is a Trinity is well-taken. But if that is what we mean, then it could be argued that no proofs exist. In these latter days it seems possible for apparently rational people to question almost everything. The argument in the *Monologion* is not likely to persuade everyone, and yet on a charitable reading, perhaps it does render the thought that God is a Trinity plausible. Anselm's proof (as we will call it) begins with certain Platonic assumptions he would have shared with his readers. And he deliberately adopts the approach of ascribing to the nature and action of God whatever is "more fitting" than not. Augustine's *On the Trinity* is constantly in the background in that, throughout the *Monologion*, Anselm brings up the operation of the human mind as Augustine had portrayed it. But the progress of the discussion in the *Monologion* is very different from that in *On the Trinity*. Anselm cites the workings of the human mind as *evidence* that it is reasonable to think God must be triune. The following is a very quick sketch of Anselm's proof.

At the beginning of the *Monologion* Anselm offers an argument for the existence of God based on the Platonic claim that the many good things we observe around us must "share in" a Highest Good and Highest Being as their source.[30] In that the things we see around us come from God, there must be Divine Ideas of these things in the mind of God. The Divine Creator is like the human artist who "speaks" within himself what he is going to make.[31] These Divine Ideas constitute a kind of expression of God, a Word by which He speaks Himself and creation. But – as discussed in the "Introduction" – Anselm, like Augustine and Aquinas, holds that all that exists is either God or what He has created. This Word, which preexists creation, cannot be a created thing. Therefore it must be God.[32] And since this Word comes from the Highest Being but is not of a different nature from its source, it is appropriate to call the source a Father and the Word a Son.[33] Father and Son are distinguished by their relationship to one another.[34] While the latter is the Word which is the Father's thinking, the Father Himself can be thought of as "memory". This is because, in the human mind, one always remembers oneself, even when one is not actively thinking about oneself. So memory is the parent and thinking is the child.[35] And certainly God loves Himself, which Love would not be possible without memory and thinking. And, since all there is is God and what He makes, and this Love is not a created thing, it must be of the same nature as God. As a "pouring out" or a "sending forth" from Father and Son, their mutual Love can be thought of as the *Spirit* of the Father and the Son.[36] We have arrived at the Trinity. Anselm takes it that he has shown that God is a Trinity, through "necessary proofs".[37] We should believe it, even if we cannot understand how it can be the case. Here Anselm turns to Augustine's analogy to help us grasp the ineffable. We may look to the human mind as a "mirror" of the divine, since it operates through memory, understanding, and love and was made by God, in His image, in order to love Him.[38] Every step is open to doubt, but if we allow certain Platonic assumptions, if we understand the human mind to be reflective of the nature of the divine, and if we share Anselm's thoughts about what is most "fitting", we may agree that he has made a plausible case for the triune nature of the divine.

A Note on Aquinas

We will discuss Aquinas briefly, since we have already looked at things he has to say about the Trinity. As noted above, Aquinas, writing a century and a half after Anselm, argues that the doctrine of the Trinity cannot be proven. However, he holds that there is nothing in the doctrine that is opposed to natural reason.[39] And he builds upon the work done by the earlier philosophers. He develops, more fully than had Augustine or Anselm, the thesis, already discussed, that the three persons of the Trinity are distinguished by their relations to one another. And he uses Augustine's analogy of the operation of the human intellect to help explain the dynamic processions within the Trinity.[40] Aquinas's approach in Question 27 of the *Summa theologiae* is especially interesting because he is concerned with responding to criticisms and misunderstandings regarding the doctrine of the Trinity. For example, it would seem that there cannot be "procession" in God, since for X to proceed from Y means for X to move outward from Y, and in God there can be no movement. Here Aquinas responds that there can be an inward procession, as evidenced by the human intellect. But can we say that in God anything is "generated"? Doesn't that imply a coming into being out of nothing? No, the term can mean a producing of something with the same nature as the producer, and so it is apt to say that the Son, Who is begotten, is "generated". But, since God is an intellectual being, shouldn't we hold that the only procession is the Word by which God thinks Himself? No, we can admit a second procession, the Spirit. Then does it follow that we must allow more, or many more, processions? No, says Aquinas. Within the divine there are only two acts, understanding and willing, and so it is right to hold to two processions, the Son and the Spirit. Question 28 of the *Summa theologiae* deals at length with the point about the three persons being distinguished by their relationships to one another. Question 29 addresses, again at length, the concern mentioned above over the use of the term "person". Aquinas follows these issues with further questions about the Trinity, such as how to understand the plurality of persons. Then he discusses each person in turn. A treatment of Aquinas's further analysis is beyond the scope of this brief introduction to the Trinity. Suffice it to say that AAA agree that, even if we cannot fully comprehend how God can be one substance or nature and three persons, the doctrine of the Trinity can be expressed in a way that does not entail contradiction. The Christian ought to commit to belief in the Trinity, and considering the image of God in the human mind can allow us at least a glimpse of this very difficult doctrine.

Notes

1 The reader interested in the discussion as it is conducted at present could check out the entry on the Trinity in the *Oxford Handbook of Philosophical Theology*. One could also look under "Trinity" in the Philosopher's Index for articles and books on the subject. Journals like *Faith and Philosophy*, *Religious Studies*, and others include work on the hard questions of Christianity in a contemporary vein.

2 See also Aquinas's *Summa contra gentiles* (SCG) Book 4.2-9. We do not find a list of biblical references to the Trinity in Anselm's main work on the Trinity, the *Monologion*. He explains in the Preface that he is attempting to set out reasons to believe that God is a Trinity without any appeal to Scripture.

3 *The Stanford Encyclopedia of Philosophy* is an excellent source for overviews of philosophers and philosophical issues written by philosophers. The articles can be difficult, in that they are written by and for philosophers, and philosophy is not a subject that lends itself to simplification for ease of access.

4 This point is not unique to philosophy. Ask a physicist what constitutes reality and the bizarreness, puzzles, and seeming paradoxes abound.

5 Augustine, *On the Trinity* Book 8.2.

6 Today the issue is clouded because "person" can refer especially to human beings toward whom we, society, have moral obligations. Thus there can be bitter debate over whether this or that human being has moral status and is a person.

7 Augustine, *On the Trinity* Book 5.9 and Book 7.4.

8 *Monologion* 79. Elsewhere Anselm, perhaps incautiously, seems to understand "person" as used of a member of the Trinity in something like the way the word would apply to a human person. See, for example, *On the Procession of the Holy Spirit* 16.

9 *Summa theologiae* (ST) 1 Q. 29.

10 ST 1 Q. 13.

11 For example, the caused and radically limited creature is good in that it reflects, or participates in, God, the absolute and infinite source of goodness. But it is still, fundamentally, the same good that God is and creatures have. See for example the beginning chapters of Anselm's *Monologion*.

12 The term "etc." stands for the attributes we properly apply to God including, for example, just, merciful, eternal, and immutable.

13 *On the Incarnation of the Word* 7. Anselm makes a similar argument concerning divine goodness in the same work, at 8.

14 See: Augustine, *On the Trinity* Book 5.5 and Book 6.7; Anselm, *Monologion* 43, *On the Incarnation of the Word* 2, *On the Procession of the Holy Spirit* 1; Aquinas, SCG Book 4.14 and 24, ST 1 Q. 28 and Q. 40.

15 Among the many themes that Augustine treats often in his works is the nature and importance of language. Book 15, the last book of *On the Trinity*, intertwines discussion of human words and the Divine Word.

16 That the Son and Holy Spirit are lesser gods than the Father was the view of the Arian heresy which prompted a great deal of rancorous debate as Christian orthodoxy was being hammered out.

17 This is how the Latin-speakers of Western Europe recited the creed several centuries after the Council of Nicaea. The original statement had not included the "*filioque* clause" – *filioque* being the Latin for "and the Son". The Greek-speakers of the East did not appreciate the "innovation" made without the entire Church met in council. The Latins argued that the *filioque* had been implied by the discussion surrounding, and following, the adoption of the Nicene Creed. Augustine's analysis of the Trinity seems to cohere with the *filioque*. This disagreement (among many other issues) contributed to the split between Eastern and Western Christendom which, though tracing back to earlier centuries, began to look permanent and official by the mid-eleventh century. Anselm attempts an explicit response to the Greeks in his *On the Procession of the Holy Spirit*. And Aquinas, too, defends the *filioque* (SCG Book 4.24). Even after the eleventh century efforts at reunion were made, and we do not know what the future holds.

18 For a discussion of the treatment of relations in the Middle Ages see Brower, Jeffrey, "Medieval Theories of Relations", *The Stanford Encyclopedia of Philosophy* (Winter 2018 Edition), Edward N. Zalta (ed.), <https://plato.stanford.edu/archives/win2018/entries/relations-medieval/>.

19 The question of whether the human being has an immaterial soul is one that has been argued from Plato's day to ours without any consensus being achieved. We will address this in Chapter 6. Here, we can set it aside in order to engage in the introspective exercise which Augustine hopes will aid us in glimpsing the Trinity.

20 Augustine discusses the triune nature of perception and the analogy on which I am focusing, the physical thing remembered, in Book 11 of *On the Trinity*.

21 Today some question whether a human being is a unified self over time. The question is interesting, but we do not need to address it in order to engage in the introspective exercise that Augustine proposes.

22 *On the Trinity* Book 14.8.

23 *On the Trinity* Book 14.12.

24 *On the Trinity* Book 15.7.

25 *On the Trinity* Book 15.22.

26 *On the Trinity* Book 15.23.

27 SCG Book 4.1, ST 1 Q. 32.

28 Aquinas allows that God might work a miracle to produce non-natural knowledge in us, but miracles are few and far between.

29 This will come up again in discussing Anselm's argument for why God "had to" become a man.

30 *Monologion* 1–2.

31 *Monologion* 9–12.

32 *Monologion* 29.

33 *Monologion* 30–42. Why not "mother" and "daughter"? "Father" and "Son" are most fitting because in human beings the "first and principle" cause of the child is the father. Aquinas explains (and perhaps this is what Anselm had in mind) that in conception the father takes a more active, and the mother a more passive, role (SCG Book 4. 11.19).

34 *Monologion* 43.

35 *Monologion* 48.

36 *Monologion* 50–57.

37 *Monologion* 64.

38 *Monologion* 66–68.

39 SCG Book 4.1.

40 ST 1 Q.27 art. 1.

2

ORIGINAL SIN

Introduction

Christianity makes an amazing claim: God – *God!* – took on human nature and became a man. Jesus, Who is the Second Person of the Trinity, was conceived in a woman, born, grew up, lived, and died – and rose! – among us here on earth. Why in the world would God do such a bizarre thing? AAA take it that the Incarnation is God's response to original sin. And so, before moving to the Incarnation, we need to address the issue of original sin. And again, the warning made at the beginning of the previous chapter is in order: Just because a doctrine seems strange at first glance, that is no reason to immediately reject it. And with original sin, there is an additional, two-part problem with trusting our first impressions. For one thing, we all suffer from very broad, very deep, ignorance. AAA hold that it did not have to be this way, for reasons that will be set out below. Secondly, all of our experiences, on which our intuitions are based, are of the human condition as it exists now. But human beings as we find them do not necessarily represent human *nature* per se. The traditional doctrine is that human beings were made good and wise by God, but the first people chose to disobey Him. This disobedience introduced a sort of dreadful "social disease" that is passed down to all human beings through the generations. We are all "infected" by original sin. Augustine explains that this Fall introduced a condition of "war" into humanity that has persisted from the dawn of human history until today. In rejecting the proper order of things, rooted in obedience to God, the first human beings set themselves – and all of their descendants – against God, against one another, and even against themselves internally. How can one be at war with oneself? AAA agree that the human being is a unity of soul and body. (This issue is discussed in Chapter Six.) At the Fall the soul, which ought to be able to govern the body effortlessly, lost its complete and painless control. Now reason fights against the desires of the body, and it

DOI: 10.4324/9781003202080-3

is only with struggle and suffering that we can resist the constant clamoring of those desires which would destroy us if we did not keep them in check. So we are at war even within ourselves. Having rejected God, human beings are inevitably drawn towards evil. We will make our own sinful choices and incur personal guilt, but even setting our personal choices aside, we suffer from a failure to conform to the good simply because we are subject to original sin.

The doctrine of original sin cannot be proven through reason alone. The Christian can accept it on faith. It is central in Church teaching and there is certainly scriptural warrant for the doctrine. The story of the first sins of Adam and Eve in the Book of Genesis describes the original Fall, and in the New Testament the point is made repeatedly that Christ's work is to save humankind from the consequences of sin. But even bracketing Church teaching and Scripture, there is reason to take the doctrine seriously. It has a great deal of explanatory power. From the dawn of human history, human beings have been vile to one another. Someone might try to explain the horrors of human-on-human violence as the product of evolution: Mammals just do that kind of thing in the struggle to get their genes into the next generation. But the merest glance at the catalog of human wickedness shows brutality and sadism and self-destruction which looks to be far in excess of evolutionary function. The Nazis may have *claimed* that the extermination of the Jews was the morally upright course required by their up-to-date and "scientific" Social Darwinism, but who would believe that? A better explanation is that the Nazis succumbed to an evil ideology. And anyone who thinks that Nazi brutality was somehow unique in human history has not looked at human history. On the other hand, human beings are, at times, capable of great moral good and fine achievements. This indicates that it is not the case that human *nature* is somehow intrinsically bad. But there is a great deal of historical evidence to support the claim that something has gone devastatingly wrong with humanity from the beginning.[1]

And now, introspect, and ask yourself "Why is it so hard to be good?" A reasonable person might well see that Plato, Aristotle, and AAA are correct in their view that the way to be happy is, in the final analysis, to behave well. And don't we all want to be happy? Being obnoxious to those around us is not likely to foster a pleasant family life or to win us many good and lasting friendships. Engaging in self-destructive behavior – even if it looks like fun at the time – will make us unhappy. Even indulging privately in mental vices like envy or hatred is likely to keep us miserable. Suppose you firmly believe that being good is the surest route to being happy. Still, isn't it surprisingly hard to stick to doing and thinking what you ought to be doing and thinking? The doctrine of original sin explains that puzzling phenomenon. AAA take it that baptism – being "washed" free from sin – makes it possible for the baptized to escape the ultimate punishment for original sin, but the effects remain.[2] Baptism is like a situation in which medicine can save the life of someone who would otherwise have died, but where it cannot entirely reverse the effects of the lingering illness. So both history and introspection suggest that the doctrine of original sin should be given fair consideration.

Modern science will not allow us to take the timeline set out in the Book of *Genesis* at face value, but AAA do not insist upon a literal reading of Scripture if that means adopting the most obvious or prima facie interpretation. Genesis says that God made man from dust. It does not say that there were no pre-human hominids involved somewhere along the creation process. At some point, there were the first human beings. We can call them Adam and Eve, but it doesn't make much difference if they referred to themselves as Og and Ogma. They were the original rational beings capable of free agency. Assuming classical theism, we can suppose that those first humans were made good by a good God. But, given the evidence of history and introspection, the claim that something went badly wrong at the dawn of human history is plausible. The first part of this chapter deals with the related questions of how a created agent, made good by God, could choose evil and why God would permit the choice. The issues of the nature of evil and of human free will will come up again and again in the course of discussing the hard questions, so it is useful to sketch out briefly how AAA address them. The second part of the chapter deals with how the original fall of the first people could so infect the rest of us.

Why Did Adam and Eve Sin?: Evil and Freedom

The problem of evil is one of the great, perennial questions in the philosophy of religion. Why does a good, omnipotent God allow all the evil that we find in our universe? Here we can barely skim the surface of the issue; just enough to ground an overview of AAA on original sin. An associated, and perhaps even more debated, question in the history of philosophy has to do with free will: Are human beings free? If so, what does our freedom consist of? What *value* does free will have, if any? Again, we can say just enough to appreciate how AAA address the question of original sin. Let us tackle evil first. AAA agree that evil *per se*, evil considered in itself, in isolation, is not some kind of a *thing*. Augustine tells us in his *Confessions* that, in his youth, he had subscribed to a religious/philosophical movement known as Manicheanism. One big advantage Augustine saw in Manicheanism was that it claimed to be able to explain why there is evil in the world. The Manicheans were cosmic dualists. They claimed to believe in something like the good God of Christianity, but also in an equal and opposite evil being. The good they associated with light and spirit, while the evil was darkness and *matter*. For all eternity these cosmic foes have been battling it out for control of the universe. Being equal, neither side can win. And human beings are the battlefield! We have souls, spirits which are a "spark of the divine", but our souls are trapped in the evil matter of our bodies. Matter, then, for the Manicheans, was the principle and explanation of evil. Why do living things suffer and fall apart and die? Because they are made of matter. Why do human beings do bad things? Because we are drawn by the evil matter of the bodies in which our good souls are trapped.

Eventually it dawned upon Augustine that the Manichean conception of God was incoherent. If the good entity is forever fighting with the bad one, but never winning, it can hardly be a god worthy of worship.[3] He abandoned Manicheanism and returned to the Christianity of his childhood. God is the absolute source of all that has any "ontological status", any real existence. God made material things, and they are good. Evil, then, cannot be any kind of a "thing". It must be a lack, an absence, a corruption, a destruction of the good. Evil can also be a disordering of what ought to be ordered, a disordering that destroys the good that the order maintained. For example, the evil choice is one that pursues the lesser and lower over the better. This is Augustine's "privative theory" of evil which Anselm and Aquinas adopt wholeheartedly. Evil is entirely parasitic on good. Even the Devil is not "pure" evil. Something with no sort of good in it at all would just blink out of being. In the universe of AAA existence itself is good, and something lacking all good is not something, but nothing.[4] So one solution to the problem of evil, the Manichean solution, is not an option for AAA.[5] But to say that evil in itself is not some kind of "stuff" leaves unresolved the problem of why there is so much wickedness and pain and suffering in a universe made by God. We turn now to "theodicy" (from the Greek for "god" and "justice"), the attempt to explain why God allows the nothingness of evil to corrupt and poison so much of our universe.

We can divide evil into natural evil and moral evil. (Different philosophers make the division in different ways. Here I divide the two species of evil in the way that will be most useful for our purposes, noting that for AAA natural evil should probably not be labeled "evil" at all for reasons explained below.) Natural evil is the pain and suffering which is not a result, directly or indirectly, of the wicked choices of moral agents. A major class of natural evil would be the suffering of lower animals where no moral agents are involved even remotely. This is a significant issue among philosophers today, but AAA are not especially concerned with it. One approach, backed by a certain interpretation of the story of the Fall in Genesis, would have it that animal suffering is the result of the sin of the first human beings. AAA do not subscribe to this theory.[6] This is due to their respect for the thought, whether along more Platonic or more Aristotelian lines, that things have natures or essences and that things are good. And the things we observe around us are all part of a good causal system. Yes, the rabbit suffers when it is eaten by the fox. But the fox could not be a fox without its fox nature which entails that it is a predator. And, given the causal system at work in the world, the rabbits could not even exist were it not for the existence of foxes. And pain and suffering serve a purpose in this overall good system.[7] AAA do not see natural evil as truly "evil" in the sense of something opposed to the good. (There will be more to say about human pain and suffering.)

Moral evil is the wickedness of the bad choices of created rational agents and the pain and suffering that results, one way and another, from those choices. The pain and suffering might be the direct result of wicked choices as when a bully beats someone up. But it could be less direct. If the builder deliberately, from selfish motives, fails to build the building up to code, then, if the building collapses due to the inherent weakness which was a result of the builder's choice to ignore the code, the ensuing pain and suffering can be attributed, at least in part, to the builder's bad choice. The builder did not intend the pain and suffering, but he is to some extent responsible for it. The consequences of moral evil can follow an even less direct path. Say that a young woman has the desire and natural talent and drive to make a unique, significant breakthrough which would lead to curing Alzheimer's in the near future. She has the funds to go to college and realize her dream, but an unscrupulous relative manages to steal her money. She is not able to go to college, she never makes the significant breakthrough, and the cure for Alzheimer's has to wait. Some pain and suffering could have been avoided had it not been for the theft perpetrated by the unscrupulous relative. It is not that the relative *intended* that more people should suffer as we wait for a cure for Alzheimer's. Still, had it not been for his evil choice, the pain and suffering would not have occurred.

AAA take the consequences of moral evil to be sweeping and universal for humanity. It was the wicked choices of our first parents that introduced original sin, the situation of "war" that infects every aspect of our lives. Had this calamitous event not occurred people could have been virtuous and wise, instead of wicked and ignorant.[8] Science, we can suppose, would be far, far more advanced than it is today. Augustine holds that government, operating as it does through deadly force, is one of the punishments due to original sin and is necessary only because of original sin.[9] AAA hold that even the terrible inevitability of death suffered by all human beings (with perhaps a couple of exceptions) would not have afflicted us had it not been for the Fall and the consequent inheritance of original sin. "The wages of sin is death" (Romans 6:23). So an enormous amount of evil – even what might prima facie look to be natural evil – can be attributed to the moral evil of that original Fall. But how could an agent created good by God make such a terrible choice? And why would God permit it?

AAA agree that the answers to both questions involve free will, its nature and its value. Early in his career Augustine wrote a book to counter the Manichean claim that evil is the result of matter entitled *On Free Will*. In it he explains that the source of evil choices is free will. It is the agent himself who is blameworthy if he chooses badly, not some dark cosmic power in which he is trapped and over which he exercises no real control. Then, was God wrong to give us free will since so much wickedness and pain and suffering results from our free choices? Of course not. Although free will allows us to choose badly, it also enables us to choose well. We could not be truly good, consciously aligning ourselves with God, if we were not free. Even if we use it badly, simply having a free will makes us splendid creatures. The dog and the horse are very good sorts of things, but they cannot be the images of God that human beings are. And a key aspect of that reflection of the divine is that, not only are we reasoning beings, but we are free agents. Free will is tremendously valuable.[10]

AAA agree that the cause of the original Fall of humanity was the free wills of Adam and Eve, and it was good for God to give them free will even if they chose badly. But what does it mean to have free will? This is a difficult question that is very much alive today. Two of the main theories at present are libertarianism and compatibilism, and, although this terminology is contemporary, the basic positions go back at least to the time of Augustine. Both of these theories have been spelled out and defended recently in a wide variety of complex and subtle versions. For our purposes here we will operate with general and rough understandings of these two theories. As I read them, Augustine and Aquinas can be seen as compatibilists, while Anselm is a libertarian. The difference between compatibilism and libertarianism leads to different answers to the question of how the first humans sinned and why God permitted it.

"Compatibilism" as we will use the term here is the position that freedom – the sort of freedom that grounds moral responsibility, praise and blame – is compatible with the ultimate cause of agents' choices being something over which they have no control. Two forms of compatibilism will concern us. One form can be called "motive compatibilism". This is the position that the agents' choices are caused by their desires, where these desires are not ultimately produced or controlled by the agent. Say that you are debating over whether to give your $20 to charity or to buy some jewelry for yourself. You end up giving to charity. Motive compatibilism explains your choice by saying that, although you wanted both to give to charity and to buy the jewelry, you gave to charity because that is what you wanted more. Your choice was determined by the strength of your particular desire. And you are not the ultimate source of that desire or its strength. Still, although you could not have chosen other than to give to charity, your choice is free. It is free because you are choosing what you want to choose. It is your own will at work. You could have chosen otherwise if the other motive had carried more weight.

Another form of compatibilism can be called "theist compatibilism". This is the view that, although God immediately, as the primary cause, causes your acts of choice, nonetheless you choose freely. (The distinction between primary and secondary causation was spelled out in the Introduction.) You choose freely because, again, you are choosing what you want through your own will. In this case, your will acts as a secondary cause, kept in being and made to choose what it chooses by God, but still, you are choosing what you want to choose. Again, it is your own will at work, although God is the ultimate cause of your will and its operations. One could be both a motive compatibilist and a theist compatibilist, that is, one could hold the view that you inevitably choose what you most desire, with God being the primary cause of your will, your desires, and your final act of choice.

"Libertarianism", for our purposes, is the position that your free choices are not caused by anything except your own choosing. It may be causally determined that you find yourself in the position of debating between giving to charity and buying the jewelry, but your final choice of giving to charity is not caused by any preceding elements over which you have no control. It was genuinely within your power to have chosen otherwise and bought the jewelry. Your choice is *a se*, that being Latin for "from yourself". The buck absolutely stops with you.

Scholars debate over whether Augustine was a libertarian early in his career. In his book *On Free Will,* he does say things that sound libertarian. For example, he speaks of the will turning this way and that, and the agent being praised for choosing well or blamed for choosing badly, when the will swings as if on a "hinge".[11] This suggests the real ability to choose otherwise which is central to libertarianism. However, later in his career, he is, beyond doubt, a compatibilist. The Manicheans had downplayed human free will, but later in his career, Augustine was confronted by a different crowd of heretics, the Pelagians. The Pelagians held that the consequences of the Fall of Adam and Eve just weren't that devastating. If people try very hard they can be good enough through their own free will to deserve heaven. We don't really need divine grace – unmerited help from God – to achieve salvation. (We will address the issue of divine grace in Chapter Four.) Here the point is that, in responding to the Pelagians, Augustine clearly subscribes to a compatibilist view of free will. Augustine holds that, contrary to the Pelagians' teaching, no one could possibly be saved without grace. Due to original sin, everyone is bound for damnation unless God steps in with grace. Grace is necessary, it cannot be merited, and it cannot be refused. He proposes that grace operates in two different ways, implying both motive and theist compatibilism. God may turn the will of the fallen agent from the bad to the good by presenting him with a good object so desirable that he cannot resist pursuing the right path. Or God may simply reach into the agent's soul and turn the will from bad to good so that now the agent loves and pursues what is right. But Augustine insists that God's gift of grace in no way interferes with, or compromises, the agent's free will. When God presents the agent with the irresistible object, it is the agent's own will that is inevitably drawn, so the agent is free on a motive compatibilist understanding. When God directly causes the agent's will to pursue the good, the agent nonetheless wills willingly as it were, and so the agent is free on a theist compatibilist understanding.[12]

Aquinas's analysis of human free will is more thorough and complex than Augustine's. Scholars disagree over exactly how to characterize his views, but a good case can be made that he agrees with the earlier philosopher: Human beings are free on a motive compatibilist, and a theist compatibilist, understanding of freedom. Aquinas does say that, when there are several different ways to achieve some desired good, we are able to choose between them. And that might sound like libertarian's insistence on open options. But when he is explaining the interactions between the intellect – the reasoning, judging element in the soul – and the will, he says that the will is moved towards its object by what the intellect judges to be the best.[13] This sounds like motive compatibilism. The textual support for Aquinas's theist compatibilism is clear. He says unequivocally and repeatedly that God causes everything including all of a created agent's acts of will, that means his choices.[14]

There are theoretical advantages and disadvantages to accepting compatibilism. An advantage of accepting motive compatibilism is that it makes a free choice intelligible in that there is an intellectually satisfying answer to the question, "Why did you choose that?". Why did you choose to give your $20 to charity? Because your desire to do so was stronger than your desire to buy the jewelry. This is an advantage that is front and center in the contemporary debate over human freedom and Augustine and Aquinas both seem to emphasize it. Even more important for Augustine and Aquinas are the advantages of accepting theist compatibilism. There are two, closely related and fundamental, theoretical advantages. AAA all understand divine omnipotence to entail that God is the source of everything that is not Himself. All created beings exist by participating in the divine being. If we understand an act of choice to be a being, something with ontological status, then it has to come from God. End of story. Moreover, both Augustine and Aquinas take it that absolutely everything that happens is actively willed by God. "Actively willed" here means more than just "permitted". They understand divine providence to entail that everything that exists and everything that happens is what God wants to have happen according to His overall plan for the world. And that includes all the free choices of created agents – "free", that is, with theist compatibilist freedom. Theist compatibilism, then, preserves the absolute omnipotence and providence, the total control of God.[15]

Why, then, did Adam and Eve sin according to Augustine and Aquinas? It helps to look at Augustine's analysis of the *very first* sins, the wicked choices by which a large swath of the angels fell, since here we have the contrast class of the angels who remained in union with God. We can see why one group held firm when the others fell. Augustine says of the bad angels that, being made from nothing, their wills could be drawn towards evil. But this is true of all the angels. Why did some fall, while others held fast to the good? It cannot be, says Augustine, that those who remained steadfast in virtue did so on their own, without extra help from God. That would mean they had made themselves better on their own, and that is absurd. The good angels did not fall because God gave them the extra grace needed to cling to the good. The bad angels fell because they were inevitably drawn to lower things and did not receive the extra grace necessary to refrain from sin.[16] And roughly the same situation applies to the first human beings. They were created good and were, originally, far more intelligent, knowledgeable, and capable than are we, their descendants. Nevertheless, they were created from nothing, and so they were able to desire lesser goods that God had forbidden, they judged these lesser goods to be the most desirable objects to pursue, and so they chose them. Their pride consists in putting their own wills ahead of God's.[17] And, consistent with the claim that everything is caused by God, God was the immediate, primary cause of their judgements and choices.

And here we see what some will take to be the disadvantage of adopting theist compatibilism. God is the cause of acts of sin. Which is not to say that God causes *evil*. Evil per se is nothing. Nor does God *do* anything evil in causing the act of sin in the created agent. That act of evil is an inherent part of the divine plan out of which God will bring good.[18] From the God's eye point of view the act of sin ought to have happened. But nonetheless, from the created agent's perspective, the created agent should not have sinned, since to sin is to disobey God. But how is it possible to disobey God, if ultimately God wills and causes the act of sin? The way Aquinas explains it is that there are two wills in God. Of course, since God is simple, there are not really two distinct and separate wills in God, but portraying the divine willing as twofold helps get the point across. There is an "antecedent will", by which God wills the good of each thing considered in isolation. The Ten Commandments, for example, express God's antecedent will for how human beings ought to behave. Someone who violates one of these commandments sins by disobeying God's will. But sometimes, when an entire situation is taken into account, it is ultimately better that the good of some particular individual be overridden. To help explain this point Aquinas gives the example of the just human judge who antecedently wishes all human beings to live. In the case of the murderer, the judge is required, both for justice and for the protection of society, to sentence the murderer to death. When all things are considered, the antecedent will of the judge should bow to his "consequent" will which takes account of the whole situation. And so with God. God antecedently wills that human beings should obey His commandments, but consequently wills the acts of sin by which they disobey.[19] But there is nothing unjust in God punishing those He has caused to sin. They sinned freely, with theist compatibilist freedom, and hence are responsible for their choices.

Augustine points out that God has made free creatures who are incapable of sinning – the good angels who never fell. And such creatures are better than those capable of sinning. Why does He not make *only* these, inevitably good, created agents? Because free creatures who are capable of sinning are good as well. Better to have two kinds of good than one.[20] But God, in his omnipotence, could simply turn people's bad wills to good so that they would always *freely* refrain from sin. True, says Augustine. Why does He not do so? God only knows.[21] We need to hold fast to the thought that God willingly allows, indeed causes, acts of sin, but brings good out of them. What sort of goods might God bring out of the evils of sinning? A lesson about justice might be learned from the punishment of the wicked. Moreover, the appropriate humility associated with repentance and forgiveness would not be possible without sin.[22] Aquinas furthers the theme: The goods of certain virtues, such as patience and justice, could not exist were it not for evil. Certain goods are more clearly recognized and appreciated when compared with evils. The order of the whole is simply better by including some evils.[23]

The most striking example of God's bringing good out of evil is Christ's Incarnation. God reaches down into our world to walk with us as one of us, and this magnificent deed is God's response to original sin. This is the doctrine of the "Fortunate Fall". In an absolute sense, it is good that Adam and Eve sinned, since it results in God becoming incarnate. The Incarnation is the "most fitting" way for God to salvage fallen humanity.[24] Would the Incarnation have happened if humanity had not fallen at the beginning? Aquinas notes that there is disagreement over the issue, but his own view is that it probably would not have happened. We learn of the Incarnation through Scripture, he points out, and Scripture consistently treats the Incarnation as the cure for original sin.[25] On the theist compatibilist view of Augustine and Aquinas, there are two ways to answer the question, "Why did Adam and Eve sin?" One way is to point to their free will, which, as a secondary cause, was drawn by pride to disobey the command of God. The other is to point to the primary cause, the consequent will of God which caused their acts of disobedience in order to realize the divine plan which includes the incalculable good of the Incarnation.

Anselm takes a different tack. He proposes a complex and careful analysis of libertarian free will and is, perhaps, the first person on the planet to do so.[26] The value of free will for created agents is that it enables them to cling to the good *on their own*, since possibly they could abandon it. This was the thought that Augustine found absurd, but Anselm takes it to be the very reason God has given us free will. Created agents participate, albeit in a very limited way, in the aseity of God and hence are true images of the divine.[27] Our acts of choice are not caused by God. We know this because people sin, and it is not possible that God causes the act of sin. Were He to do so, He would have to do so willingly. But to sin is to will what God wills that you not will. So it is logically impossible that God could cause the act of sin.[28] What about Aquinas's suggestion of the two wills in God, the antecedent will by which He issues commands and the consequent will by which He causes created agents to disobey those commands? Aquinas is writing more than a century after Anselm, and Anselm offers not the faintest hint of this double will in God. The theory of the double will suggests a kind of deception on the part of God. Aquinas would likely insist that God is not subject to anthropomorphic moral judgments on our part. It is not clear that Anselm would agree. Anselm insists that Christ, as God, could not possibly will to lie.[29] The tenor of Anselm's thought suggests that he would find the theory of the two divine wills distasteful. The bottom line is that God does not cause the act of sin. It is up to the created agent alone to cause the act of sin, and this means that it is up to the created agent alone to refrain from sin.

Libertarianism, as I have described it, insists upon the aseity of the agent's choice. Moreover, the agent must confront open options. Like Augustine, Anselm discusses the fall of the angels. This is the purest instance of a free choice, and so the bare mechanics of choosing can be laid out. Moreover we can compare the fall of the bad angels to the steadfastness of the good. Anselm argues that God provided the angels with open options. Since their motivations come from God, if they were motivated in only one direction their choices would be up to God rather than themselves. God provides two, competing desires, the desires for justice and for benefit. They want to hold fast to justice and obey God. Obeying God means pursuing only those benefits that God wills that one should have or have at the time. No one, says Anselm, wills anything unless he believes it to be beneficial, to be something that will make him happy.[30] But the angels also want to pursue some benefit that God is not yet ready for them to have.[31] The bad angels won't wait. They choose to disobey God. In a sense impatience constitutes the first sin, though, of course, the sin is also pride in that the bad angels put their own wills ahead of God's. But how could they possibly have done that? That they were made from nothing and were *able* to choose badly does not explain the choice, since the good angels were in exactly the same situation. Anselm does not adopt Augustine's answer that God gave the good angels the necessary grace that He withheld from the bad. Why then did the bad angels choose badly, while the good angels did not? Only because they chose![32] Any attempt to offer a further explanation in terms of the nature of the angels, their wills, their motivations, and their situation must implicate God in the sinful choice, and Anselm will not have that. Anselm does not say much about the sins of Adam and Eve, but he says enough to show that he takes the same analysis of created freedom to apply. Why did Adam and Eve choose to sin when they could have remained in obedience to God? There is no explanation beyond their own wills making the choice.[33]

Does this mean that Anselm has rejected the classical theist view of omnipotence on which God is the cause of every existent being besides Himself? That would signal a deep inconsistency in Anselm's work. He is aware of the problem and proposes a solution. God is the absolute source of the existence of everything that has any ontological status, any real being, in a free choice. He is the cause of the agent, the agent's will, and the competing desires which produce the situation in which the agent chooses between options. What is up to the created agent, and *all* that is up to the created agent, is which of the God-given desires is pursued to the point of actual intention, such that the other desire ceases to exercise motive power. This "perwilling" as Anselm calls it, is what the free choice consists in, but it does not add anything to the sum of things in the universe. The choice itself has no ontological status beyond that of the God-given desire which constitutes it. God is the cause of all that *exists*, but He is not the cause of all that *happens*.[34] Certainly God can bring good out of evil. Anselm, like Augustine and Aquinas, understands the Incarnation to be occasioned by the Fall of Adam and Eve and the dire condition they bequeathed to their descendants. But God did not cause the Fall. Rather, He permits it because the only way to abolish sin would be to shut down the free will that enables the created agent to be good on its own. And free will is incredibly valuable.[35] Moreover, God knows how to incorporate the original Fall, and the other free choices of created agents, into His plan.[36]

That God is not the cause of all that happens is a striking thing to say among classical theists. It undermines God's absolute sovereignty. Anselm can respond that God Himself set up the system this way because created free will is such a great good. Still, one has to accept that God is not absolutely in control of all that happens. And that is a hard theoretical pill for the classical theist to swallow. But the alternative is to say that everything, including every created agent's "free" choice to sin, is caused by God. And this might suggest that the narrative of Christian history is a play written by God in which, ultimately, He is acting all the parts. It is a story God is telling to Himself. Given how "real" sin seems to be, and given all the pain and suffering caused by moral evil, this, too, is difficult to accept. Even more difficult is the thought that God rewards and (especially!) punishes in accord with people's choices, which choices He Himself has caused. Here, I take it, we have a deep theoretical conflict where there is no middle ground. It is not likely to be resolved by further argument, more general information, or a more careful reading of Scripture. You are free to choose either approach, but with what manner of freedom, Heaven knows.

The Transmission of Original Sin

AAA agree that the dire consequences of the first sin of Adam and Eve are transmitted to their descendants down the generations. As Aquinas points out, Scripture says that the wages of sin is death, and as far as we can tell pretty much everyone dies.[37] Furthermore, AAA have no doubt that Scripture is clear that original sin is the problem that God became incarnate to solve. And, as I argued above, the doctrine of original sin has a lot of explanatory value. But how does that transmission work?[38] Even more fundamentally, how do new human beings come to exist? Of course, we don't get a baby without sexual union (setting aside the Incarnation). But if the human person is a unity of soul and body, are both soul and body produced, on the level of secondary causation, by the actions of the parents? Or is it just the body that is thus produced, while the soul is newly "implanted" by God? Augustine debates the question in Book 10 of *On the Literal Meaning of Genesis* but does not come to any final conclusion. Anselm does not weigh in, probably because he died before he got to write a proposed treatise on the soul. Aquinas holds that each new soul is immediately created by God.[39] AAA agree, then, that the existence of each human *body* can be traced back causally to Adam and Eve. Augustine is not sure that an analogous claim can be made about the soul, while Aquinas holds that it certainly cannot. So none of the three argues that original sin is transmitted from souls to souls through the generations. It is the causal chain of physical bodies starting from the first human beings that is the conduit for original sin.[40] But how?

Augustine holds that the "seed" from the parents is "stained" due to the manner of its transmission. After the Fall, he argues, sexual activity inevitably involves an element of the disorder of sin. This is true even of the morally acceptable sexual activity within marriage. Had our first parents not sinned, human beings would have reproduced sexually, but they would have had complete control over their bodies. The soul, having its proper authority over the body, would have effortlessly exercised its control over *all* of the movements of *all* of the parts of our bodies, as it now controls only some, such as the hands and feet. But the first sin introduced a state of "war" even between soul and body.[41] We know from Augustine's *Confessions* that he knew what he was talking about when it comes to the power of sexual lust. His claim is that, even within marriage, an element of uncontrolled, and hence disordered, desire must be present for sexual activity to take place. A "stain" of corruption is thus transmitted to the body of the new child, and the body infects the soul.[42] Augustine even suggests that the sins of our more immediate forebears might add to our burden of guilt.[43] The "stain" of original sin is then a sort of palpable darkness transmitted bodily, through sexual intercourse, down the generations.

Anselm understands the transmission of original sin in a very different way than does Augustine. Anselm's view is that there is nothing sinful about appropriate sexual acts within marriage and so the condition of sin is not transmitted through the act of conception.[44] The first human beings were created by God with a desire for justice. But, like the angels, they were also able to desire some benefit that they ought not to have, at least not then. By opting to pursue the unjust desire they "expelled" the desire for justice. The desire for justice was the desire to will in accord with the will of God, and that meant to curb their desires for mere benefits and pursue only those good things that would be appropriate at the time. When the desire for justice is lost, appetite runs wild.[45] This is a version of an old, distinguished, and plausible claim. It is the theme of Plato's *Republic* and crops up in Augustine's work over and over. Failure to control one's desires leads to ruin. Anselm explains that once the desire for justice is lost the will is so overrun with the "weeds" of innumerable inappropriate desires that the desire for justice cannot be regained without divine grace, which grace must link the sinner to the remarkable sacrifice of Christ. (Grace is the subject of Chapter Four.) The Fall, then, is Adam and Eve's throwing away the "original justice" in which they were created. But why should the rest of us suffer for what our first parents did?

Anselm's view is that, not only did God give the first people the desire for justice, He gave them the amazing ability, as part of their reproductive nature, to pass along the desire for justice to their children. Having thrown the desire for justice away, Adam and Eve did not possess it to hand down to their children and their children's children. So it is not that original sin is an existent stain passed from parent to child. It is "nothing" in the sense of being the lack of a desire for justice which Adam and Eve ought to have kept and bequeathed to their children. He offers the analogy of parents who are given great wealth, but then squander it so that they are impoverished. This leaves their children impoverished as well since the parents threw away the wealth that they should have guarded and handed on.[46] (Had Adam and Eve not sinned, Anselm suggests that their descendants would have been so "confirmed" in justice that they would not have been able to sin.[47] Aquinas explicitly disagrees, arguing that it would be unreasonable to believe that the children of Adam and Eve would be better than their parents.[48]) Anselm notes that someone might wonder why God, at the Fall, didn't just scrap the human family biologically descended from Adam and Eve and start over with new human beings who might hold fast to justice. Why would God choose instead to salvage the family of Adam and Eve through the Incarnation? The answer, according to Anselm, is that God loved the particular human family He had made, and He valued its reproductive nature, and so, rather than destroy it, He chose to save it by sending His Son.[49]

Aquinas is influenced by both Augustine and Anselm but adds a somewhat different slant on original sin. He agrees with Augustine that original sin can be seen as a "stain" passed down the generations through sexual union. For example, in arguing that Christ is not afflicted with original sin, he says that the contamination is handed down due to the lustful desires involved in ordinary procreation.[50] And he notes, citing Augustine, that since the corruption of original sin is transmitted through generation, the human powers associated with conception, like the power to reproduce and the sense of touch, are especially infected.[51] But he often follows Anselm in the thought that what Adam and Eve lost in the beginning was "original justice", where original justice is the proper ordering of human beings to God, to one another, and within the self. But he proposes a somewhat different picture than had Anselm. Yes, humanity is infected by original sin because Adam threw away the desire for justice and so did not have it to pass on to his progeny. [52] But Anselm, as noted above, focuses on the value of the *biological* unity of humankind descended, by physical reproduction, from Adam. Aquinas, on the other hand, places more emphasis on the unity of human *nature*. We are all members of the human species, and the nature itself is damaged in the sin of the first humans. And thus we share the guilt initiated by Adam. He offers a telling analogy. Because we share a nature, human beings are a community, analogous to the various parts of a single body. The hand by which the murderer kills is not guilty in and of itself as a hand, but it shares the murderer's guilt as moved by the will of the murderer. Adam's will can be said to act in humanity as the murderer's will moves the hand, and so the original sin can be imputed to all of us. [53] For Anselm original sin was just the lack of the original justice which Adam and Eve should have passed on to their descendants. In spite of its devastating effects, "it" has no being at all. It is just nothing. This distinguished Anselm somewhat from Augustine for whom original sin seemed to be more of a palpable darkness.

Aquinas, in speaking of the damage to human nature as a "stain" sounds more like Augustine. This can be underscored by comparing the analogies from ordinary human business that Anselm and Aquinas offer. Above I noted Anselm's point that we probably would not find it an injustice on the part of God or society if children are poor because their parents squandered the great wealth they had been given. We might blame the parents and feel sorry for the children but, even today, you just don't get to inherit your parent's lost riches. The children simply lack what their parents should have preserved to pass on to them. Aquinas proposes a different analogy, arguing that someone who is not blameworthy in himself, may, considering his family origin, be reproached. From his birth, he may suffer under a family disgrace due to a crime committed by one of his ancestors. [54] This "family disgrace" seems more of a positive stain than the lack of wealth in Anselm's example. Aquinas emphasizes the "stain" imagery but then goes on to express the stain as a loss of the brightness that belongs to the human soul. [55] So perhaps we might read Aquinas's analysis of the transmission of original sin as an attempt to reconcile Augustine's thought that original sin is handed down as a stain from person to person with Anselm's theory of original sin being the original loss, and subsequent absence, of original justice. But Aquinas does seem to go beyond both of his predecessors when he says that, since we all have human nature, all of humanity sins through Adam's will in the same way that each part of a person's body can be said to sin through the will of that individual person.

One tentative suggestion to explain this difference could be that the earlier philosophers are more Platonic, while Aquinas is more Aristotelian, when it comes to how things have the natures that they have. Augustine and Anselm can be seen as exemplarists: The natures of things exist as ideas, "exemplars", in the mind of God and, in order to explain how this cat is a cat, or that human being is a human being, one points to the exemplar and to the relationship of participation or reflection by which the creature "shares in" the idea in God's mind. If the human nature that makes the human being a human being exists mainly as an exemplar, then it is incoherent to suppose that the nature itself, the idea in the mind of God, is stained or corrupted. Aquinas's "hand" analogy which aims to explain how the individual descendant of Adam suffers from original sin because of the shared *nature* does not work well on exemplarism. Aquinas, of course, believes that God is a rational Creator, and so there are ideas in God's mind of what He will make. But, as an Aristotelian, Aquinas takes it that natures exist robustly in the created things.[56] The catness of the cats exists in the cats. It is made into individual cats by their particular matter. Human nature exists in the human beings, individuated by their matter. Since Adam was the first human being, there is a sense in which all of human nature existed in him. So the nature itself might be corruptible in a way that the divine idea of humanness could not be.[57] But however we analyze the transmission of original sin, it is hard to dispute the claim that all of humanity is infected and corrupted in such a way that we tend to be drawn to evil. Thank goodness there is a cure for our dire situation. It begins with the Incarnation, the subject of the next chapter.

Notes

1 G.K. Chesterton writes, "Certain new theologians dispute original sin, which is the only part of Christian theology which really be proved." *Orthodoxy*, "The Maniac" 1.

2 Aquinas, *Summa theologiae* (ST) 1–2 (First Part of the Second Part) Q. 85.

3 *Confessions* Book 7.2.

4 *Confessions* Book 7.12; Anselm, *On the Fall of the Devil* 9–11; Aquinas, *Summa contra gentiles* (SCG) Book 3.7.

5 Versions of cosmic dualism pitting the good spirit against the evil matter – which evil matter especially includes the human body – seem to crop up periodically in Western thought. The Albigensians in southern France and northern Italy in the twelfth century are an example.

6 Aquinas, ST 1 Q. 9 art. 1 ad 2.

7 Augustine, *On the Literal Meaning of Genesis* Book 3.16.
8 The question of what would have happened if some later progeny of a sinless first couple were to sin is an open one which probably does not have an answer.
9 *City of God* Book 19.17.
10 Augustine at the end of Book 2 and beginning of Book 3 in *On Free Will.*
11 *On Free Will* Book 3.1.
12 *On Grace and Free Will.* (This is only one of Augustine's several anti-Pelagian works.)
13 SCG Book 3.10.12, ST 1 Q. 82 arts. 1–3, especially art. 3, reply to objection 3. In Article 4 Aquinas says that in a sense the will moves the intellect, but he concludes (reply to objection 3) that ultimately the recognition of the good by the intellect comes first. See also ST 1–2 Q. 9 art. 1.
14 SCG Book 3. 66–67 and 88–89, ST 1 Q. 105 arts. 4–5.
15 Augustine and Aquinas make these points in the texts cited above as evidence of their theist compatibilism.
16 *City of God* Book 12.7–9.
17 *City of God* Book 14.13.
18 When Aquinas is giving his Five Ways to prove the existence of God, he raises the existence of evil as the first objection to God's existence. In response he cites Augustine's claim that God allows evil in order to bring good out of it (ST 1 Q.2 art. 3 ad 1).
19 ST 1 Q. 19 art. 6 ad 1.
20 *On the Literal Meaning of Genesis* Book 11.7.
21 *On the Literal Meaning of Genesis* Book 11.10.
22 *On the Literal Meaning of Genesis* Book 11.11.
23 SCG Book 3.71.
24 Augustine, *On the Trinity* Book 12.10; Aquinas ST 3 Q.1 art. 2.
25 ST 3 Q. 1 art. 3.
26 As Augustine expresses the Pelagians' views they sound like they are assuming something like libertarianism, but as far as we know they did not work out a careful analysis of free choice. Anselm certainly rejects Pelagianism.
27 *Cur Deus Homo* Book 2.10.
28 *On Freedom of Choice* 8.
29 *Cur Deus Homo* Book 2.17.
30 *On the Fall of the Devil* 12.
31 *On the Fall of the Devil* 13 and 14. "Justice" is "rightness of will kept for its own sake" and "rightness of will" is willing in accord with the will of God (*On Truth* 12).
32 *On the Fall of the Devil* 27.
33 Anselm discusses the Fall in Book 3 of *On the Harmony of God's Foreknowledge, Predestination, and Grace with Free Choice* (*De concordia*) where the main topic is reconciling human freedom with the necessity for grace. Contemporary critics of libertarianism take the absence of an explanation for the agent's choosing to lead to the "luck" problem: If an agent's choice is not explained by preceding facts about the agent, isn't it just a matter of luck that the agent chooses this over that? Anselm's approach suggests that the critics have the situation backwards. Rather than insisting that it is character that causes choice, choice is what creates character. But the choice is not "lucky" in the sense of something that happens to you. It is your own doing.
34 The discussion of "perwilling" is found in *On the Fall of the Devil* 3. On the point that God causes all that *exists* in a choice but does not cause the choice see *De concordia* Book 3.11–14.

35 Anselm, unlike Augustine and Aquinas, can pursue a version of the "Free Will Defense": God must permit moral evil since the only way to prevent it is to eliminate created free will. Compatibilists cannot make this move, since on compatibilism God could prevent all moral evil without undermining free will.

36 Anselm reconciles human freedom with divine predestination in Book 2 of *De concordia*.

37 SCG Book 4.50. 1.

38 Some might ascribe the transmission of original sin to perverse social practices: Society is a mess and so children are corrupted by their environment. But that problem could be alleviated by social progress. AAA take it that the corruption of original sin goes deeper, inevitably infecting even newborn children.

39 ST 1 Q. 90 art. 3.

40 Aquinas holds that some new person miraculously formed by God from new human flesh would not be afflicted with original sin (ST 1–2 Q. 81 art. 4).

41 *City of God* Book 14.16–26.

42 *On Marriage and Concupiscence* Book 1.24.27, *On the Grace of Christ and Original Sin* Book 2.45. In the contemporary setting sperm and egg could be united in a petri dish without lust. Would Augustine think that the new human being must be infected with original sin? If not, that seems a strike against his view.

43 *Enchiridion* 56.

44 *On the* Virgin *Conception and Original Sin* 4.

45 *De concordia* Book 3.10, *On the Virgin Conception and Original Sin* 5.

46 *On the Virgin Conception and Original Sin* 28.

47 *Cur Deus Homo* Book 1.18.

48 ST 1 Q. 100 art. 2.

49 *On the Virgin Conception and Original Sin* 17 and 23.

50 ST 3 Q. 31 art. 4 ad 3 and art. 7.

51 ST 1–2 Q. 83 art. 4.

52 ST 1–2 Q. 83 art. 3. Here he cites Anselm by name. There is a somewhat different emphasis, though, since Aquinas is clear that the original justice is a supernatural gift from God, a special grace transcending human nature per se. Anselm does not say that the original justice is "supernatural".

53 ST 1–2 Q. 81 art. 1 and Q. 83 art. 1.

54 ST 1–2 Q. 81 art. 2 ad 5.

55 ST 1–2 Q. 86.

56 Augustine and Anselm might say this as well, but for them the natures in the creatures exist only as reflections or participations in the exemplars.

57 If Christ is fully man as well as fully God, how is His human nature not infected with original sin? Aquinas responds that the damage done to the nature involves the loss of grace, but as God Christ cannot suffer that lack. Also Christ receives His nature in a different way than the rest of us do. SCG Book 4.52. 9–11, ST 3 Q. 31 art. 1 ad 3.

3

THE INCARNATION AND ATONEMENT

Introduction

All of humanity is infected with the terrible disease of original sin. Thankfully there is a cure. The Second Person of the Trinity, the Son, became incarnate, that is, He joined Himself to a human soul and body in order to effect the reconciliation of humanity to God, the Atonement. ("Atonement" can be read as literally "at one-ment", in this case, God and humanity "made one" through being reconciled.) As the Council of Chalcedon insisted, Jesus Christ is fully God and fully man, one person with two natures, divine and human. He was conceived within the Blessed Virgin Mary, grew up, spread the good news that the Kingdom of God was at hand, then suffered, died, was buried, rose again on the third day, and ascended into heaven. What a strange story! Early in the history of Christendom numerous theories were advanced to "shield" God from the claim that He really became Incarnate. Aquinas offers a lengthy review of many of these theories in Book 4.28–38 of the *Summa contra gentiles*.[1] A main motivation for many of these theories was the view that matter in general, and human bodies in particular, are nasty. Surely God would not stoop to be joined with a human soul and body! Moreover, intellectuals had worked long and hard to free humanity from the silly worship of animals, stones, wooden idols, obnoxious gods such as Zeus and his companions, and the stars of the sky. And now the claim is being made that the God of Jewish monotheism became flesh and is to be worshipped in the person of Jesus of Nazareth. It is no wonder that people impressed with aspects of Jesus's work and His claim to be the Son of God nonetheless had a hard time accepting that He was God incarnate. Wouldn't it be better to say that God only *appeared* to take on flesh? Or, alternatively, that Jesus wasn't fully or exactly God? Maybe he was a slightly lesser divinity than the Father? Or just a very good man, used by God? These suggestions, and myriad variants on

DOI: 10.4324/9781003202080-4

them and other theories besides, were proposed in the early centuries of Christianity, hence the need for the Council of Chalcedon. Of course, non-conciliar views continued to circulate after the council, and even today one runs into contemporary versions of these ancient heresies (as we will call them).

AAA are all committed to the understanding of the Incarnation that was codified at Chalcedon. Christ is one person with two natures, He is fully God and fully human. And since AAA understand the human being to be a unity of soul and body, there is no way to avoid the conclusion that the Son "assumes" – incorporates into Himself – both a human soul and a human body. (It is not that God finds an already existent human person and then adds him to Himself. That would entail the destruction of that person, qua person. The body and soul of God incarnate come into being at Jesus's conception.) AAA are confronted with two very hard questions. The first is: Why in the world would God choose to save humanity through such a roundabout, not to mention distasteful, process? God is omnipotent and perfectly rational. Couldn't He just save the human race by fiat? It is, at least at first glance, hard to see why He would choose incarnation. One might respond, "Don't ask! That's just what He did. End of story." But AAA, each in their own time and place, are confronted by people who reject Christianity and who are quick to point out what looks to be the unseemly weirdness of the claim that God assumes a human nature. AAA believe in the Incarnation on faith, but charity to those who do not believe (and deepening the faith of believers) demands that they try to explain why God would choose such an unlikely method for redeeming humanity.

A second question, possibly even harder than the first, is *how* God is incarnate. Can any sense be made of the claim that God incarnate is one person with two natures? The two natures are wildly different to the point that the properties of one seem to be the opposite of the properties of the other. (We will use the "property" talk, even though strictly speaking God does not have properties). For a single person to be both God and man seems to entail that that person is both A and not-A in the same way at the same time. The person Who is Jesus Christ is both omnipotent and limited in strength, eternal and in time, ubiquitous and limited in space. AAA take it that even if we cannot see *how* God is incarnate, we must believe *that* He is incarnate. But they do not ask us to accept contradictions and they have a way to address this apparent paradox. Christ is not A and not-A *in the same way* at the same time. Rather He is one way *as divine* and another *as human*. We can call this the "qua" move, *qua* being the Latin for "as". This is not an easy doctrine, but it allows for the Incarnation without contradiction, and there is an analogy to help us achieve some understanding. But first, why would God choose to become incarnate as the way to save humanity?

Augustine on Why God Became Incarnate

AAA agree that God, being omnipotent, could have brought about the salvation of humanity in a number of different ways, but they all go on to argue that the way God actually did choose to do it – through assuming a human nature and living and dying and rising among us – was the most appropriate and effective way to achieve the goal.[2] Anselm insists that we must not ascribe the least unfittingness to God and His actions, and that means that in a sense the Incarnation "had to" happen. As we will see, he goes so far as to claim to be able to *prove* the Incarnation to non-Christians who initially find it absurd and unwholesome. Neither Augustine nor Aquinas explicitly says that it was "necessary" for God to redeem humanity through the Incarnation, but nor do they allow that God could *actually* act in a less appropriate and less effective way than He might. All three, then, hold that there is at least good reason for God to become incarnate, and, indeed, all three propose that there are many reasons, including reasons that are hidden from us.

Augustine discusses reasons for the Incarnation in *On the Trinity* especially in Book 13. Here he is concerned to show that human beings can be truly happy. But unalloyed happiness requires belief in the immortality of the whole person, soul, *and body*. (The afterlife is discussed in Chapter Six.) Many philosophers had argued that the human soul is immortal. Plato is a prime example. But the thought that the body could die and yet be resurrected and immortal is a thought that such philosophers found laughable. Augustine grants that the Christian would believe in the resurrection of the body based on faith. But one reason for the fittingness of the Incarnation is that if God took on a human nature, soul and body, and rose from the dead, then that makes it easier to believe that each individual human person, and the *whole* human person, may be immortal. Further, by becoming incarnate God emphasizes the great value of human beings, especially to those who might question it because they take a dim view of matter. Moreover, God teaches the virtue of humility by subjecting Himself not only to association with a human nature, but by being treated shamefully in that nature. And He teaches obedience, even to being unjustly killed. All of these reasons suggest that the Incarnation serves as an example regarding human nature and human morality. The Incarnation teaches that the resurrection of the human body is possible, that human beings have a special dignity, and that human beings ought to be humble and ought to be obedient to God. Another line of justification that Augustine introduces is the thought that, being without sin, Christ does not owe any debt to God, but being incarnate allows Him nonetheless to "pay the debt" for the rest of us. Scripture includes this debt language but does not go into detail on how it works, and Augustine does not offer any extended discussion of what payment of the debt entails.

Augustine offers a further explanation, suggested by earlier theologians, for just how it is that humanity is saved by Christ's crucifixion.[3] When the original human beings sinned, they placed themselves under the power of the Devil. Augustine says that Satan had "just rights" to enslave humanity after the Fall.[4] But Satan loses the right to control human beings by committing his own injustice when he helps to engineer the death of the one human being who, being sinless, does not deserve to die. Christ tricks Satan and frees humanity by allowing Himself to be killed unjustly. Augustine even uses the colorful metaphor of the Cross being a "mousetrap" baited with Christ's blood![5] We can call this explanation the "Augustinian" theory of the Atonement. Augustine's theory was a popular one for centuries after his death, but Anselm roundly rejects it for reasons to be discussed below. The theory seems to have fallen out of favor after Anselm's rejection. Aquinas rehearses many of Augustine's arguments for the appropriateness of the Incarnation, but he does not include the "mousetrap" thesis. In our own times, however, the Augustinian theory – at least a fictionalized version modeled on it – has been revived and entered into popular culture. C.S. Lewis's *The Lion, the Witch, and the Wardrobe* tells the story of a traitor justly held by the evil witch and freed only when the witch unjustly puts to death, in place of the traitor, a willing and innocent victim, Aslan, the Christ figure in Lewis's *The Chronicles of Narnia*.

Augustine has provided a list of reasons why it was fitting for God to assume a human nature. And yet someone skeptical about the Incarnation – for example a monotheist who finds the doctrine demeaning to God – might note that apparently God could have achieved any of the supposed divine aims of the Incarnation without going through the bizarre, nasty process. Couldn't God just resurrect some good human person to demonstrate the possibility of resurrection and the dignity of the whole human person? Couldn't God just make a new human being not descended from Adam and possessing original justice? And then that new human being could bait the trap for Satan and, being sinless, could pay the debt he did not owe. Anselm, centuries later, develops the debt payment thesis into his extended proof that the Incarnation was necessary; *only* God having become a human being can reconcile fallen humanity to Himself.

Anselm on Why God Became Man

C. S. Lewis notwithstanding, Anselm finds Augustine's theory of the Atonement seriously mistaken. In his *Cur deus homo* (*Why God Became Man* or *Why a God-man?* We can abbreviate it CDH.) he spells out what he takes to be wrong with Augustine's proposal and offers a theory of his own which he says shows that God could not have failed to become incarnate. Anselm finds it absurd that the Devil could have any "just rights" over humanity. God is the absolute standard for justice and what it is to be just is to freely conform to God's will. The Devil is a greater sinner even than human beings and cannot mount any *just* claims to anything. People get confused, says Anselm, because it is just that humanity should be punished, and God permits Satan to do some of the punishing, but it does not follow that the Devil himself has any "just right" to do so.[6] In a separate work, *Meditation on Human Redemption,* which is a prayerful sketch of the *Cur deus homo* argument, Anselm attacks a facet of the Augustinian theory that he had not mentioned in CDH. He finds the "mousetrap" element offensive. God did not intend to deceive the Devil. He did not even intend for the Devil to deceive himself. He only *permitted* the Devil to deceive himself. God is Truth and deliberate deception on His part cannot be key to the divine plan for human salvation. One interesting, and perhaps wholesome, consequence of Anselm's rejecting and replacing Augustine's theory is that it removes Satan from center stage in the drama of human salvation.[7]

Why, then, according to Anselm, did God become man? CDH is a dialogue between Anselm and a friend and fellow monk, Boso. Scholars debate whether or not Anselm really intended CDH as a proof of the Incarnation, but the textual evidence suggests that he did. (In Chapter One, on the Trinity, I briefly discussed Anselm's qualified understanding of what a proof entails.) At the end of the work, Anselm has Boso exclaim that the argument ought to convince non-Christians.[8] As usual with Anselm it is probably best to read the work as aiming at two goals: to deepen the understanding of the committed Christian and to help to convert the non-Christian. At the beginning of the dialogue Boso points out that non-Christians such as Jews and Muslims find the Incarnation absurd, and more than absurd, it is gross. It is absurd to claim that the one, purely immaterial God should join Himself to a human nature, including a human body. It is even worse to hold that, in that human nature, God should suffer and be crucified. But maybe worst of all is the claim that

God incarnate was conceived and grew inside a woman.[9] Anselm sets out to show that it had to be this way.

Anselm expects his readers, including Jews and Muslims, to accept three premises. First, he assumes that there is a perfectly good God who inevitably does what is best.[10] Second, God made humanity to be happy. This is easy to prove since we all do want to be happy, and a perfectly good God would not make creatures with such a deep and fundamental desire if He had not intended it to be satisfied.[11] But, thirdly, something has gone badly wrong with humanity from the dawn of human history. Our sinful condition is such that we do not deserve to be, and really *cannot* be, happy. (Jews and Muslims could well accept the first two premises, but they might have doubts about the third.) God, being good, would do something to rectify the situation.[12] Why does He not simply forgive humanity? After all, says Boso, God tells us to forgive those who wrong us. Anselm argues that simple forgiveness – forgiveness without some appropriate action on the part of humankind – would not be the best. For one thing, God is the absolute standard for justice. He is Justice Itself. Simple forgiveness would entail God treating the sinful as if they were sinless. That might be merciful, but it is unjust. If, *per impossibile* ("through some impossibility") God could act unjustly, that would destroy justice throughout the universe. Whereas you and I can be excused if we mistakenly elevate mercy to the point of injustice, God is uniquely situated such that He cannot be unjust.[13] Moreover, humanity is a mess. Human beings in our fallen condition are not the kinds of things that can enjoy the happiness for which we were intended. We need to be "cleaned up" before we can be reunited with God. Simple forgiveness would not produce the needed effect.[14]

Furthermore, sin constitutes an attack on the "honor" of God, a rejection of God as the highest being, source of all, and standard of justice. So humanity needs to "pay the debt" owed to God. Some object to the "debt" language. Is our salvation some kind of financial transaction? Anselm's argument can go through if we emphasize, instead, the need to close the distance between us and God through Christ's atoning work. But the debt language is scriptural and sets a down-to-earth tone which makes Anselm's argument more accessible, so we will stick with it. Not only *should* humanity pay the debt owed to God but, if we are sorry about our situation and truly want to be reconciled with God, we would *want* to pay the debt.[15] One could argue that insistence on the payment of the debt, by requiring action on the part of human beings, shows more respect for human dignity than simple forgiveness.[16]

So it is better for the debt to be repaid. The problem is this: God is infinite. Sin, rejecting God, thus incurs an enormous debt. Anselm is dreadfully clear about the terrible weight of sin, and not just the first Fall or some major, dramatic sin. He asks Boso whether or not it would be right to take the merest glance forbidden by God if by doing so you could save the whole created universe.[17] Boso says no, one should not turn away from God, even slightly, in order to save the universe. And this is the correct answer. The reason the universe has value is because it participates in the divine nature. It is incoherent to place the universe over God in importance. This means that the debt humanity owes is huge – too large for any mere human being to be able to pay it.[18] With all of the reasons Augustine gives for the Incarnation it seems that the same values might be achieved had God chosen to create a new, sinless, merely human person to provide the example, teach the lessons, and undergo the unjust crucifixion. Anselm explains why only God can pay the debt. It is just too big for any mere human to pay.

But the debt has to be paid by those who owe it. This means human beings and, in fact, human beings descended from Adam and Eve. It is best that the debt be paid and the only one who can pay it must be both God and a member our human family.[19] The debt is paid out of gratuitous love by the freely chosen obedience of Christ to God. Unlike the rest of us, Christ does not owe God a death. He chooses to die as a way of paying the price for our redemption.[20] But how can the death of one person – even God incarnate – open the way for atonement for all the rest of us? Anselm holds that there is a sort of unity in the human family such that one member of the family can justly pay the debt for all the members. It is the unity of biological kinship. And this is why God adopted the messy process of being conceived in, and born of, a woman. God could have avoided that unseemly element of the story by assuming a newly created, perhaps adult, human nature. But that version of Christ would not have been a member of the family of Adam and Eve, so He would not have the sort of unity with the rest of us that enables Him to pay our debt.[21]

There is one more step involved in the salvation of the individual human being. The individual is not simply the passive recipient of Christ's payment of the debt for humanity. Each of us needs to deliberately embrace Christ's saving work on our behalf.[22] This requires divine grace. Grace is a complicated issue to be addressed in the next chapter. Anselm works to reconcile the necessity of grace with some input from human free will. The point here is that the individual human being needs to align himself with Christ and Christ's payment of the debt. The debt must be paid by humanity and only God can pay it. Thus it is *necessary* that God become incarnate as a human being.

It is interesting that Christ's *resurrection* does not play a role in the CDH argument. It is not the resurrection *per se* that achieves the atonement. Undoubtedly Anselm would agree with Augustine that belief in Christ's bodily rising from the dead would help Christians to hope for the immortality of the whole person, soul and body.[23] And Christ's life gives human beings a crucial example of how to live.[24] Anselm explicitly says that there are many reasons why God should become incarnate and that his argument captures only one.[25] But that one argument, he believes, ought to convince the non-Christian monotheist.

Aquinas on the Appropriateness of the Incarnation

Aquinas's discussion of the value of the Incarnation is not framed as a proof, but he does say that it was "necessary" in the sense that it was the best and most convenient way to achieve the goal of humanity's salvation.[26] Aquinas lists a number of reasons for the Incarnation, some drawn from Augustine and Anselm, and some not found in the earlier philosophers.[27] Aquinas proposes a general value for the Incarnation that neither Augustine nor Anselm mentions, the difference likely being due to the fundamental distinction between the more Platonic epistemology of the earlier thinkers and Aquinas's more Aristotelian epistemology. Aquinas is an empiricist. He holds that our natural knowledge begins with our senses. In this life, we have no natural direct access to the transcendent God. We can prove that God exists, but only by arguing from the observable effects around us to their unobservable divine cause.[28] It is reasonable to believe things about God on faith, but the teaching itself comes through sensible instruction. If God Himself takes on a sensible human body, then His teaching is likely to be more powerful and efficacious.[29] Moreover, with no direct access to God in this life, human beings might despair of ever being able to "see" Him. This would be terrible since the whole goal of our lives is eternal beatitude in the presence of God. But if God descends to our level, allowing (at least some of) us to be with Him even in this earthly life, then we know that He is not absolutely unapproachable, and our hope in eternal beatitude is supported.[30]

Aquinas does borrow several of Augustine's reasons for the Incarnation. They include that belief in Christ as God incarnate can strengthen our hope in the immortality of the whole person, soul and body. Aquinas goes on to add that Christ had to take on flesh that was capable of suffering and death, because if He had assumed some sort of "superior" flesh, as some critics suggest, that being more appropriate for God, then we might fear that our own frail bodies could not be resurrected as Christ's was. And taking on flesh like ours enables Christ to serve as a better example of virtue, especially the virtue of humility.[31] As Augustine had said, the Incarnation also underscores human dignity. Moreover, it is appropriate that the Devil's power over human beings should be defeated by right-eousness.[32] What Aquinas does *not* borrow from Augustine is the theory that Satan had "just rights" over humanity which he lost when he committed the injustice of helping to engineer the unjust crucifixion. Anselm had apparently discouraged later thinkers from embracing Augustine's "mousetrap" proposal.

Aquinas also includes the thought that God must become man to pay the debt humanity owes to God due to original sin. Augustine had mentioned this idea in a sentence, whereas Anselm develops it into two lengthy books. Aquinas devotes a little more time to it than had Augustine, though he gives it only a few sentences. His treatment of this "debt" argument in his *Summa contra gentiles* differs slightly from that in the *Summa theologiae* which was written later. In the later work, he adds a point which brings him closer to Anselm. A key issue for both Anselm and Aquinas is why the payment of the debt had to be made by God. Why wouldn't some other innocent victim, perhaps a newly created, sinless human being, suffice? In *Summa contra gentiles* Aquinas explains that only God can pay the debt because He is paying for the entire human race. The debt is so huge only God can pay it because it is the accumulated debt of all human beings.[33] Anselm gives a very different reason: Sin – any sin – incurs an enormously weighty debt because it is a rejection of God, Justice Itself. In the *Summa theologiae* Aquinas repeats the point that no mere human being could make satisfaction for the harm done to human nature and all of humanity. But he adds that a sin against God has a kind of infinity because it is an affront to the infinite majesty of God. Satisfaction, then, as Anselm had said, requires the sort of infinite power that only God possesses.[34] Finally, similar to both Augustine and Anselm, Aquinas holds that in addition to the many reasons he has offered for why it is best that God save humanity through assuming a human nature, body and soul, there are certainly other advantages that transcend our human ability to grasp. So, while one might believe in the Incarnation on faith, there are numerous reasons to consider it a fitting divine response to original sin.

How Is the Incarnation Possible?

AAA have argued that the Incarnation is an appropriate, perhaps even necessary, way for God to salvage the human family. But how is the position of the Council of Chalcedon even possible? How can one person have two natures, especially when those natures are so wildly different, one divine and one human? In the early Church a plethora of unorthodox views attempted to solve the apparent paradox by denying that Christ was one divine person with two natures. For example, might it not be easier to grasp if we say that the two natures are joined such that the divine becomes human, or the human divine? Or perhaps the two are mixed to form a third nature, different from either? Chalcedon rejected all attempts to deny that Christ is one person with two natures. Anselm insists that the impossibility lies with the unorthodox suggestions: the divine and human natures are such that it is inconceivable that one could *become* the other, or that the two could be mixed.[35] Moreover, someone who did not fit the Chalcedonian description could not accomplish a key aim of the Incarnation. As Anselm and Aquinas set out the debt payment view, it is only humanity that owes the debt, but the debt is so enormous that only God can pay it. If Christ were only God, or only man, or some third thing, neither God nor man, then the debt could not be paid.[36] How, then, to make sense of one person with both a divine and a human nature?

Christ is a person, the Second person of the Trinity, the Son or Word of the Father. The Son "assumes", joins to Himself, a human nature, a human soul and body. The Son does not assume a human "person". Two impossibilities follow that suggestion. One is that there would have been two persons in Christ, which cannot happen since a person is an individual and there cannot be a person who is two persons. The other is that the "person-ness" of the human person would have been destroyed. But God would not destroy a person. The human soul and body are assumed by the Son, and the only person involved is the Son. That human soul and body are the human nature of the Son and come into being at Christ's conception.[37]

But how can one person have different, even opposing, properties? AAA answer with the "qua" move. "Qua" is Latin for "as". Christ has certain properties as divine, and others as human. So, qua divine, Christ is immortal, while qua human He can be killed. Qua divine Christ is eternal and ubiquitous, qua human He is located in time and space.[38] Remember, says Aquinas, that "Christ" refers primarily to the person who is the Son, so we can say "Christ is divine, immortal, eternal, etc." without qualification. It is equally correct to say, "Christ is human, mortal, born during the reign of Caesar Augustus, etc." but "…in his human nature" should be added.[39]

AAA propose the analogy of a human person's soul and body to help make the idea of the union of Christ's disparate natures closer to human experience.[40] The soul is (distantly) analogous to the Son, and the body to the human nature. AAA all hold that the human person is a unity constituted by a soul and a body. So the thought that one person may have two basic aspects or features is not outlandish. The soul is superior to the body, containing the most important feature of the human person, the intellect, and the soul animates and guides the body. It is appropriate, says Aquinas, to think of the body as an "instrument" used by the soul. But not, he hastens to add, an "external" instrument like an axe or a saw that exists outside of the person and can be taken up or put down at will. The body is an instrument which is proper and conjoined to the person. This hand is *my* hand.[41] The restoration of the body to the soul at the resurrection is (distantly) analogous to the Son's assumption of a human nature.[42]

AAA, adhering to the inerrancy of Scripture, are confronted with a number of puzzles regarding the Incarnation as Jesus's sayings and doings are recorded in the Gospels.[43] What of Christ's knowledge? He possesses both a divine and a human intellect. As divine He is certainly omniscient. Anselm argues that, while it was useful for Christ to adopt mortality in His human nature, there would be no point in adopting ignorance and so Christ is omniscient, even in infancy – no "qua divine" involved.[44] Aquinas, too, attributes an amazing amount of knowledge to Christ, even in infancy, and even in His human nature. The *Summa theologiae* Part 3, Question 9 offers a much more complex answer to the question of Christ's knowledge than we find in Anselm. It is too complex to spell out thoroughly here, especially because some points depend on Aquinas's well-developed and involved epistemology. But we can sketch some of the important outlines. Christ has two intellects, one divine and one human. The divine intellect is omniscient without qualification, and so Christ is omniscient. But Christ's human intellect must operate as human intellects do. Anselm had not emphasized this point, and, again, perhaps this is due to the difference between Anselm's more Neoplatonic epistemology and Aquinas's Aristotelian empiricism. Given the two intellects, Christ has both divine and created knowledge. Ordinarily, human knowledge begins with the senses. Data is received through observation of the world around us and then the active aspect of the intellect operates on the data to produce knowledge – that is, theoretical understanding. The knowledge thus obtained can be called "acquired" knowledge. God could work a miracle, even on an ordinary human being, such that He could impart knowledge immediately to the knower. This is "infused" knowledge. So the human intellect is capable of possessing both acquired and infused knowledge, and Christ's human soul does have both kinds of knowledge.[45] Aquinas says that even qua human, Christ has infused knowledge of all species – essentially He knows all of science. And He knows all that is revealed by God. He knows all that has happened, is happening, or will happen. Yet, His human intellect cannot know some things because they are simply beyond human capacities. Christ's human intellect beholds the beatific vision as the blessed human beings enjoy it in the afterlife, but it does not comprehend the divine essence. This is knowledge beyond the reach of any human being, even the human nature assumed by the Son.[46] Does Christ's human intellect possess all this knowledge from conception? Aquinas, like Anselm, seems to say yes. There can be no ignorance in Christ's human soul. And Christ receives His human soul at conception.[47]

Was Christ omnipotent? Yes, in His divine nature, but not in His human nature. Aquinas explains that Christ's human soul does not exercise perfect divine power even over His human body. It is not in the nature of human souls to do that.[48] But in two senses omnipotence can be attributed to Christ even in His human nature. First, the human soul and body of Christ are assumed by the Son as His instrument. He can use His instrument however He wills, thus the instrument can exercise omnipotence. Second, Christ, qua human, wills two kinds of things. He wills what is to be brought about by human power and He wills what is to be brought about by divine power. His human will is entirely in accord with His divine will and so whatever He wills to be done by divine omnipotence, even though it is willed qua human, is done through divine omnipotence.[49]

But this brings up the vexed question of Christ's will. Here Scripture poses an obvious problem for the qua move: Sometimes the Gospels seem to say that Christ qua human is willing *in opposition to* the Father, when the will of Christ as Second person of the Trinity is one with the will of the Father. For example, before His capture and crucifixion, Christ prays not to have to suffer what He knows is coming but says "not my will, but thine, be done". Is there an opposition between the wills of Christ qua human and qua divine? If Christ is one person can He really have two wills that can will contrary things? Aquinas carefully develops an answer that is found earlier in a brief discussion by Anselm. In the course of *Cur deus homo* Anselm explains that Christ's human soul can will – that is, desire – in accord with human nature, inevitably wishing to avoid suffering. But this human desire does not undermine the fixed and rational choice to undergo the suffering that is necessary for the salvation of humanity.[50] Aquinas makes a similar point. Christ, qua human, has a natural and appetitive (or sensual) will which naturally shrinks from pain, but He also has a will that obeys His reason and which overrides the natural will when it would lead Him astray. Any human being has these wills, but with the rest of us, it is not a foregone conclusion that the rational will has the last word.[51] (Aquinas phrases his point in terms of several "wills" but presumably there is a single will exercised under several different aspects.)

The (roughly similar) answer that Anselm and Aquinas give to the question about tension between the divine and human wills in Christ raises a further problem. Both hold that Christ is free, apparently without qualification: Crucifixion is "a death He freely accepted". They both allow that He is free qua divine and free qua human. But they both hold that Christ's human will must accord with the divine will. How, then, is His human will free? Here Anselm and Aquinas give interestingly different answers grounded in their different views of free will. (See Chapter Two for their theories of human freedom.) Aquinas, adopting a compatibilist approach, holds that the human agent, *any* human agent, can will freely even though all of his acts of willing are caused immediately by God as the primary cause (the cause that makes things exist). As long as the human agent is able to choose and do what he wants he is free. So there is no more problem in insisting that Christ's human will is free, is necessarily good, and is directed by the divine will, than there would be in making the same claim about any of the saints.[52]

Anselm opts for a different position. He has argued that, in order for merely human agents to have the sort of freedom that can ground moral responsibility, they must confront genuinely open, morally significant choices. They must have the option to choose to hold on to the good on their own, or to abandon it. The core of freedom is aseity, the ability to choose "from oneself". But everything that the human agent has and is comes from God. Even the desires which motivate him come from God. In order to cling to the good on his own, a se, the created agent must have the option to abandon it. Divine freedom works differently. God's freedom does not require open, morally significant options because God exists absolutely a se. What He wills He wills "from Himself" in the most ultimate sense. What about Christ's human will? Anselm holds that it is impossible for Christ to sin. His human will accords perfectly with His divine will. This is because, qua human, He desires only the good. Why? Because His divine nature has given his human nature only the desire for good. It is true that Christ does not confront competing motivations and open options, but nonetheless, even qua human, He is free. He wills absolutely *a se*, from Himself, because He is one person. Qua divine He gives the unyielding desire for good to Himself qua human.[53] This does not mean that Christ's human willing is totally alien to the willing of other human beings. Those in heaven inevitably will the good, but freely, since they have it "from themselves" that now they see only the good to desire.[54] Christ's human will can thus be entirely in accord with His divine will and yet be free.

The Incarnation is a mystery. We cannot expect to wrap our minds around it or explicate it with analytic clarity. But the qua move made by AAA allows them to express the nature of Christ without contradiction. That is an impressive feat. According to AAA the Incarnation is possible, and it is the most fitting way for God to salvage sinful humanity. But by itself, it is not enough. Human beings need to commit to Christ and His saving work. But we are steeped in sin. How can we turn to Christ and be saved? AAA agree that that will require divine grace, and grace will be the subject of the next chapter.

Notes

1 Aquinas here is heavily indebted to Augustine's *On Heresies*.
2 Augustine *On the Trinity* Book 13.9.12; Anselm *Cur deus homo*; Aquinas *Summa contra gentiles* (SCG) Book 4.54–55.
3 The proposal is spelled out in *On the Trinity* Book 13.12–14.
4 *On the Trinity* Book 4.13.17.
5 Sermon 130.
6 CDH Book 1.7.
7 I say "wholesome" because a fascination with the Devil can be unhealthy. Anselm's theory of the Atonement insists that human salvation is a matter between God and humanity.
8 CDH Book 2.22.
9 CDH Book 1.3.
10 Here I can offer only a bare outline of the argument.
11 CDH Book 2.1.
12 CDH Book 2.4.
13 CDH Book 1.12. Anselm meditates on the relationship of divine justice to divine mercy in *Proslogion* 9–11.
14 CDH Book 1.19.
15 CDH Book 1.24.
16 If you had stolen money from someone and then felt sorry and wanted to repay it, wouldn't it show that they respected you more if they let you repay it than if they just said "Nevermind"?
17 This is a thought experiment. Anselm does not suggest that God really might destroy His creation.
18 CDH Book 1.21.
19 CDH Book 2.6,8, and 9.
20 CDH Book 2.18–19.
21 CDH Book 2.8. In our times this understanding of family unity may be received with skepticism, but perhaps that is an indictment of our society rather than a problem with the *Cur deus homo* argument.
22 CDH Book 2.16. Anselm here tells a parable to explain how those alive before or after Christ's crucifixion can nonetheless embrace it as payment of their debt.
23 CDH Preface and Book 2.3.
24 CDH Book 2.18.
25 CDH Book 1.2.
26 *Summa theologiae* (ST) 3. 1. 2.
27 SCG Book 4 Chapter 53 offers a list of criticisms of the doctrine of the Incarnation, and then Chapters 54 and 55 answer the criticisms.
28 All of Aquinas's "Five Ways" to prove the existence of God work this way (ST 1 Q. 2.3.).
29 SCG Book 4.55.7. (The topic is why God did not assume an angelic nature rather than a human nature.)
30 SCG Book 4.54.2.

31 SCG Book 4. 55.14 and 21.
32 ST 3.1.2.
33 SCG Book 4.54.9 and 55.22–23 and 27.
34 ST 3 Q. 1 art. 2 ad 2.
35 CDH 2.7; Aquinas ST 3 Q. 4 art. 2.
36 CDH 2.7.
37 SCG 4.43–44.
38 Augustine *On the Trinity* Book 1.13; Anselm CDH Book 1. 8; Aquinas SCG 4. 27.4, ST 3 Q.16 art. 4.
39 Aquinas ST 3 Q.20 art.2.
40 Anselm CDH Book 2.7; Aquinas SCG Book 4.34.22 and 41.9. In the latter text Aquinas attributes the analogy to Augustine from a work called *Against Felician*. Subsequent scholarship concludes that this was not actually written by Augustine. But a clouded pedigree does not undermine the value of the analogy.
41 SCG 4.41.9–11, ST 3 Q. 2.
42 ST 3 Q. 2 ad 2.
43 Augustine does not go into depth on how the "qua" move should be spelled out.
44 CDH Book 2.13.
45 ST 3 Q. 9.
46 ST 3 Q. 10.
47 ST 3 Q. 15 art. 3. On Aquinas's Aristotelian biology, this is different from other human beings who are "ensouled" through successive souls until the body is finally in a condition to receive a rational soul (ST 3 Q. 33 art. 2 ad 3). The thought of all of Christ's immense knowledge possessed from conception is likely to strike the modern reader as strange. We tend to think that mind activity is closely associated with brain activity. An embryonic, fetal, or infant brain does not seem up to holding all the knowledge which Aquinas attributes to Christ's human soul. One might deny the modern understanding of the mind/brain relationship or argue that Christ is just different. Or perhaps the infused and acquired knowledge accumulates slowly in Christ's human soul as the brain grows. This seems consistent with the Chalcedonian statement of the nature of Christ.
48 ST 3 Q. 13 art. 3.
49 ST 3 Q. 13 art. 4.
50 CDH Book 1. 9.
51 ST 3 Q.18.
52 ST 3 Q.18 art.1 ad 1.
53 CDH Book 1.9–10 and Book 2.10.
54 *On the Fall of the Devil* 25 and *De concordia* 3.4.

4

GRACE

Introduction

The disease of original sin is terrible and pervasive, and the further ac-
cumulation of individual sins is overpowering. The situation is so dire
that God becomes incarnate and is crucified in order to rescue humanity.
But the process of atonement does not end when Christ's earthly work
is done. The individual human being cannot be saved unless he turns to
God, embracing the saving action of Christ as the means to his salvation.
And how is that turning possible when the individual is so steeped in sin?
Augustine, Anselm, and Aquinas (AAA) agree that only extra, direct help
from God – grace – can enable the conversion.[1] Divine grace is absolutely
necessary and cannot be deserved. It is grace that initiates the process
whereby the sinner can turn to God, implanting the first seeds of the
necessary faith in Christ. And this initial grace opens the way for a further
grace that bestows the subsequent perseverance to enable the wayfarer (as
we might term those journeying through this life) to cling to God until
the end. The saved thus receive "grace for grace".[2] Augustine solidifies the
arguments for the necessity of grace in his disputes with the Pelagians,
churchmen of his day who denied that grace is necessary for salvation.
We will look first at this seminal debate wherein Augustine's victory es-
tablished the view accepted by most Christians, Catholic and Protestant,
from his day to ours: Salvation requires faith in Christ as our Savior, and
faith in Christ is possible only through unmerited grace.[3]

But if divine grace initiates the process of the salvation of the individual, and provides the perseverance to see the journey through to the
end, where is there room for human free will that might allow for moral
responsibility? AAA agree that the need for, and reception of, grace does
not conflict with the individual's free will. But their explanations for how
grace and human freedom interact differ based on their different understandings of the nature of human free will. (Their positions on free will

DOI: 10.4324/9781003202080-5

are sketched in Chapter Two). Augustine and Aquinas are compatibilists, while Anselm is a libertarian. We will see how that impacts their attempts to reconcile freedom and grace. Finally we will address a series of questions: Would grace have been necessary if humanity had not sinned in the beginning? Why does God extend His grace to some and not to others? Can grace be lost? Do you know if you have grace? Can the rest of us know if you have grace? What are the gifts of grace? For those who have grace, do all have it equally?

The Pelagian Controversy

Early in his career Augustine had argued against the Manichean heresy which held that matter is the principle of evil and that people do bad things because their good spirit is trapped in an evil body. Augustine insisted that people choose as they do because of their free will.[4] But later he confronted a new challenge to orthodoxy, Pelagianism. This was an especially personal challenge to Augustine since Pelagius and his followers claimed Augustine's own defense of free will in support of their position. Augustine, in response, wrote a series of books against Pelagius. In brief, Pelagianism held that the original Fall of Adam and Eve had not done quite the destruction that we attributed to it in Chapter Two. Humanity is not so damaged that grace is necessary for salvation. It is ultimately up to our free will whether or not we are good enough to achieve eternal beatitude. Augustine argued that in that case humanity would not need Christ's saving work. God's incarnation, crucifixion, and death were pointless. And that conflicts with Scripture and cannot be allowed.[5] Indeed, all goods come from God. Augustine often repeats St. Paul's question (Corinthians 4:7): What do you have that you have not received?[6] The Pelagians are fundamentally mistaken when they claim that it is one's free choices that determine one's final destiny.

Here we should pause for a short historical digression. It will help to show how Christian doctrine is developed and also to explain Augustine's rejection of Pelagianism in its various forms. Pelagius was clever. He was asked to explain his views at a hearing before several important churchmen, and he stated that, contrary to what his enemies said, he did indeed hold that grace is necessary for salvation.[7] The tribunal found nothing to object to in his views and was prepared to permit him to continue to teach his position as one accepted by the Church. Augustine, who had read Pelagius's books, would not let him get away with what was essentially a deception. Augustine pointed out that it is crucial to understand just what is meant by "grace". In a sense, of course, one could hold that all of creation is "grace", the gratuitous gift of existence to creatures. In

his books Pelagius had sometimes understood "grace" to be God giving humanity its human nature, including free will, and sometimes he
had understood it to be God forgiving sins and delivering the Law –
commandments to guide human life. What he did *not* mean by it was direct
help from God to the individual to turn him from his immersion in evil
back towards God. And that, according to Augustine, is what the Church,
following the Scriptures, meant by the "grace" that enables salvation.[8]

Pelagius and his followers offered several lines of defense. Some said
that immediate help from God was indeed necessary for salvation, but the
gift could be initiated by the individual freely choosing the good. That
is, grace is necessary, but it can be merited. This view is sometimes called
"semi-Pelagianism", but Augustine held it to be roughly the same as, and
certainly no better than, Pelagianism pure and simple. If we can, on our
own, *deserve* that God should give us the grace that leads to heaven,
then, again, we are not so deeply immersed in sin and Christ need not
have died.[9] Pelagius attempted to revise his position by claiming that he
had never said that many people were *in fact* good enough through their
own free will, without preceding grace, to merit salvation or to initiate
the reception of grace. Maybe it happens that no one has actually been
sufficiently good on their own. The view, said Pelagius, is simply that it
is *possible* that one could be good enough through their own free will to
merit salvation or to prompt God's giving the necessary grace. Augustine
does not accept this qualification of the view. If Pelagius is saying it is even
possible for someone to be so good on their own as to deserve heaven or
merit the grace to get there then, again, he is denying the full impact of
original sin on humanity. And to deny the extent of the disease of original
sin is to minimize the need for the cure – Christ's saving work.[10]

Pelagius makes one more move and that is to suggest that he and his
opponents can just agree to differ. Reasonable people could defend either
side in the debate, and it is not a matter where taking one side or the other
would undermine one's faith. Thus Augustine should leave him alone.
Tolerant as this sounds, Augustine cannot go along. Scripture is clear, he
holds, that it is Christ's death which pays the debt for our sins – original
sin and personal sins. The entire Christian story is wildly distorted if humanity is not so bad after all and Christ's work is not so crucial. Augustine
repeats that it is central to the faith that in order to turn to Christ we
must have grace and cannot deserve it. Thus the Church leaders should
withdraw their statement that the teaching of Pelagius and his followers
is acceptable.[11] The modern reader may object to Augustine's attempting
to either silence or convert Pelagius, but it is important to remember that
Pelagius wants to claim the mantel of orthodoxy within the Church. He
insists that his view is approved by the Church. And, representing himself

as a spokesman for Christian doctrine, he is teaching his views to many of the more simple faithful who are not in a position to study and evaluate them.[12] Augustine hopes Pelagius will abandon his theory. If he does not the Church leaders should officially and decisively withdraw their support from Pelagius so that he cannot spread his harmful view as being within the fold of Christian orthodoxy. Pelagianism was condemned as heretical by the Council of Carthage in 418. For Anselm and Aquinas the thought that grace might be unnecessary, or that it could be merited, is out of the question, and that is what the Catholic Church and most traditionally-minded Christians have held from Augustine's day to ours.

Reconciling Grace and Free Will

If grace begins the process of the individual's salvation, and grace supplies the perseverance to stay the heaven-bound course, does free will have any role to play? AAA all insist that grace and free will work together in the salvation of the human individual. Augustine and Anselm both begin their discussions of grace and free will by setting out the biblical texts that could suggest that only grace is at work and also those that could suggest that it is human freedom that decides the question of the individual's salvation. And Aquinas's work on grace and free will is full of biblical citations, some emphasizing grace and some emphasizing free will. It is important philosophically, and to do justice to Scripture, to show that freedom and grace can be reconciled.

The task is not hard for Augustine and Aquinas. As I explained in Chapter Two, both are compatibilists regarding free will. As long as it is your own will choosing and pursuing what you want, you are free and an appropriate subject for praise and blame. Perhaps your desires are not of your own making, and you inevitably choose and pursue what you most desire, but if you are choosing and doing what you want, that is freedom. And it may be that God causes your choices and subsequent actions, but He does so through your own will, and so you are free. If you are forced to act against your will – maybe you are tied down or there is a gun to your head – you are not free, but that your choices and actions are the product of determining causes, primary (God) or secondary (created) or both, does not undermine freedom. Thus God's turning the will of the sinner back towards Himself, and bestowing perseverance until death, does not conflict with the free will of the elect (those God has chosen to save). The elect choose God and choose to pursue the good because that is what God makes them choose. But it is nevertheless their own wills choosing.[13]

But it is common for people not immersed in philosophy to have "libertarian intuitions"; a free choice must involve real options and be "up to" the agent in some ultimate sense. Even in Augustine's day, the worry arose that his teachings on grace minimized the importance of free will to the point where no one could be held morally responsible for their choices and actions.[14] On the assumption that God judges the good and the bad, this raises questions about divine justice. And it might also encourage moral laxness. That is, if you believe that you must inevitably sin unless God gives you grace so that you inevitably avoid sin, then it seems pointless to struggle to find the moral strength to cling to the good. Whatever you actually end up choosing and doing was caused by forces beyond your control. This worry did not die down after Augustine's death. The respective roles of grace and free will was debated throughout the Middle Ages and was one of the thorny questions that split Western Christendom between Catholics and Protestants in the early modern period. Indeed, the worry is with us to the present day.

Anselm, I believe, offers a plausible, libertarian analysis reconciling grace and free will, without allowing the faintest hint of Pelagianism. Grace is necessary, and it cannot be merited. It is necessary to provide those first seeds of faith, and it is necessary for the perseverance required to see the journey through to the end. But, according to Anselm, what grace consists in is God's restoring to the human will what was lost through original sin, that is original justice. Adam threw away his desire for justice and so was unable to pass it along to his offspring. Subsequent generations have free will, in the sense that they have the *ability* to cling to justice. Unfortunately, the knowledge of, and desire for, justice is no longer part of the cognitive and motivational makeup of the human being. The will could will justly if it possessed justice, but justice is lost to it. Analogously, you might have the intrinsic ability to see a mountain, but if there is no mountain there you will not see it. Divine grace restores the lost knowledge of, and desire for, justice and also the ability to persevere in that knowledge and desire.[15]

However, we know from the experience of Adam that one receiving these things can fail to persevere in justice. The person who has received the desire for justice and the ability to maintain it to the end can reject justice. Upon the reception of grace, the motivational structure of the human agent returns to that of humanity in the original condition. The agent faces open options, and it is up to the agent which he chooses. Though the agent desires to conform to the will of God, another desire can arise, the desire for some inappropriate benefit. It is up to the human being to cling to justice. But, as did Adam and Eve, the agent can "eject" the desire for justice by choosing the inappropriate benefit.[16] And since the agent who has received grace can abandon the effects of grace there is a role for human freedom to play. It is a very small role – just holding fast to the God-given grace or not – and so Anselm can give the proper answer to St. Paul's question: What do you have that you have not received? Nothing! All goods come from God.

Anselm offers a simple, but telling, analogy. Suppose someone is naked and a benefactor gives him not only clothes to wear but also the ability to keep wearing the clothes. That this person is clothed is due to the benefactor. But now suppose that the person freely takes the clothes off and throws them away. That he finds himself naked is his own doing. This is because, in accordance with Anselm's libertarian analysis of free will, the agent had open options – to keep or discard the clothes – and it was ultimately up to the agent himself which he chose. That means that if he freely keeps the clothes – he does not take them off and throw them away when he could – then he gets a little credit for being clothed. Not much, since all he did was not reject what he was given. Still, that counts for something. And so with grace. All of the good things in the process – the restored desire for, and ability to keep, justice – are caused by God, but the human agent could abandon these good things by choosing badly. Thus grace and free will are reconciled.[17]

Were Augustine and Aquinas to consider Anselm's analogy they would object to its point. If the naked person represents the fallen human being and the benefactor represents God, then, in the final analysis, the newly clothed person, if given the ability to keep the clothes, cannot choose on his own to discard them. If he freely wills to keep the clothes it is the benefactor, God, who causes that choice. God gives the initial grace, God gives the perseverance, and it is up to God whether or not the human agent continues in grace until death. Augustine's and Aquinas's view does raise the difficulties with divine justice and moral laxness. Anselm's position, on the other hand, suggests that God's sovereignty is not absolute; human agents have some genuine input into how things go in the universe. And that is a problematic conclusion as well. It is easy to see why the debate over grace and free will has continued to trouble the Christian community.

Further Questions Pertaining to Grace

Would human beings have needed divine grace if there had been no original sin? The answer is yes if we take grace in the broadest sense; grace is the gratuitous benefits which God bestows on creatures, and that includes their existence. Augustine and Anselm focus on the grace that helps us recover from original sin and so they do not pose the question concerning the need for grace in the hypothetical, unfallen condition. Aquinas, though, argues that if we take grace to be extra, supernatural, divine help, beyond God giving us existence and our natural capacities, then we would need grace even had the first people not sinned. His position derives from two related themes in his work which set him apart from Augustine and Anselm. As we have noted, Aquinas is an empiricist. All of our natural knowledge, that is knowledge not bestowed miraculously by God, begins with observation of the physical world around us. Secondly, it is important to distinguish carefully between the natural and the supernatural. As it applies to the human condition, the natural pertains to our lives here and now as rational animals on planet Earth. *Natural* knowledge is the knowledge that we can gain through the natural capacities of the human being starting with sense observation. The supernatural applies to the things beyond nature, angels and God, for example. The supernatural includes the actions of these beings in our physical world. God can bestow miraculous knowledge on a human being and that knowledge would then be "supernatural" knowledge. With regard to grace, the important distinction is between our natural goal in life and our ultimate, supernatural goal. Our natural goal is to achieve happiness, which is to flourish as human beings, here and now. In order to achieve our natural goal we can direct our natural observational and reasoning powers to key questions: What kind of thing are we human beings? How can our kind of thing actualize its potentials in the right way to achieve happiness? But our ultimate goal is eternal happiness with God in the afterlife. God transcends the physical world, so our natural capacities are not able to guide us to this ultimate goal. And this would have been the case, Fall or no Fall. The inability to grasp the ultimate goal cognitively, and hence to pursue it, is a consequence of the limitations of human nature itself. And so, says Aquinas, even if humanity had not been affected by original sin, we would need that extra, supernatural help from God. As things stand with fallen human beings, we need grace both to recognize the ultimate goal and also to allow us to recover from original sin.[18]

Another question arises from the view, which AAA all agree is found in Scripture, that God does not give grace to everyone. Why not? The distinction cannot be that some merit grace while others do not since grace is unmerited. Aquinas explains that those who do not receive grace have put some kind of obstacle in the way. But that is the situation with all of us since we all inherit original sin. It is grace that removes this obstacle from some and not from others.[19] So the question remains, why does God bestow saving grace on some and not on others? The answer is painfully simple: That is just what He chooses to do. There is nothing special about any particular human being that would provide a reason for God to give that person grace and not the next person. Is the divine choice arbitrary? No, say AAA, but it is inscrutable from the human perspective.

We cannot expect to comprehend the will of God. But isn't it unjust for God to give grace to some and not to others when all alike are infected with original sin? No, they say. All human beings are mired in sin and, absent grace, deserve hell. Divine justice would not require that anyone be saved. Divine mercy tempers justice, and so God chooses some on whom to bestow grace. But why these and not those is beyond the capacity of human beings to grasp.[20]

Would it seem more just to say that God bestows saving grace on everyone? Augustine and Aquinas cannot make this move, since they hold that if God bestows saving grace the receiving agent is saved. And they believe, with solid Scriptural backing, that hell is not empty. So there are some on whom God did not bestow the necessary grace. Anselm *could have* accepted this proposal without any structural damage to his system. He *could have* said that God bestows grace on everyone, but hell is populated by those who have freely chosen to reject it. He does not make this move. Perhaps he considered it contrary to Scripture or too distant from Augustine's position. Today some embrace universalism, the thought that God ensures that everyone ultimately enjoys the beatific vision. This seems a more pleasant position than that advanced by AAA, but it is difficult to square with Scripture and has no roots in traditional Church teaching. Moreover, if Anselm is right that robust libertarian freedom contributes to our being images of God there may be a reason for God to respect the choices of individuals who consistently choose badly. (More on hell in Chapter Six.)

The issue of God giving grace to some and not others is especially difficult in the case of infants who die before they can reason and act on their own. Some receive the grace of baptism, which removes the stain of original sin, and these infants go to heaven. This shows, says Augustine, that grace is unmerited since an infant cannot have done anything to deserve the grace of baptism.[21] Some are not baptized and go to hell. AAA take this to be the proper interpretation of Scripture, but they certainly do not treat it as a pleasant conclusion. Anselm cautions us that we should not let our feelings of compassion get in the way of accepting a consequence for which there are the strongest arguments. He does go on to say that it is reasonable to suppose that unbaptized infants suffer less than would someone who had committed their own personal sins.[22] Aquinas, too, argues that unbaptized infants who die will suffer less, both physically and mentally, than will those who have achieved the age of reason and committed their own sins.[23] Today the Catholic Church holds that we may legitimately hope that God in His mercy will find a way to salvation for unbaptized children.[24]

Insisting on the necessity of grace in the case of adults, do AAA consider one's actual deeds unimportant regarding one's relationship to God? Grace will imbue a person with faith in Christ, but is an inactive faith enough? No. Mere belief is not the sign of salvation. Augustine quotes the Letter of James (2:19); the demons believe and tremble. An adult cannot be saved without good works. It is good works that earn the eternal reward. But the good works themselves are the result of grace.[25]

Can grace be lost? That is, can one receive the grace which rescues us from original sin and turns us back to God, but lose it such that one does not persevere to the end of one's life? Anselm, as discussed above, answers, "Yes". It is possible to throw away the graciously restored desire for justice by willing some unjust benefit. Thus, for Anselm, the individual's free will has a decisive role to play in his destiny. Augustine and Aquinas agree that grace can be lost.[26] Someone who has received grace may not receive perseverance, or having received grace and perseverance, may not receive perseverance to the end of life. And, just as with the initiating of grace, it is up to God to give the perseverance. If God does not do so, then the human being, restored through grace, will fall back into a condition of sin. God, of course, can then give grace to that person yet again, if He chooses. As Augustine notes this means that we can never be sure of who is bound for glory and who is not. And this is, perhaps, a wholesome consequence in that, according to Augustine, it follows that we should try to treat our fellow human beings with respect, and hope they will be saved since any of them could turn out to be saints.[27]

We cannot know, from the outside, who has received grace and especially the grace that causes perseverance to the end of life. But can we know for ourselves, from the inside, if we have received saving grace? Augustine holds that we can have good evidence of having received grace and perseverance, and that is that we do not find following God's commandments painful or difficult.[28] But no one can be absolutely certain that he is chosen to be among the elect. The danger of failing to persevere is always there. And this is a good thing, says Augustine, since otherwise one might succumb to pride.[29] Aquinas asks the same question: Can we know we have grace? One might think we should be able to recognize grace since it is in our souls that grace would appear. We know it immediately when we have gained some new knowledge, and the reception of grace would be similar, would it not? Aquinas answers in his characteristic careful, analytic style. There are three ways one might suppose one could know that one had grace. If God has revealed to someone that they are the recipient of saving grace, then they can have certainty. Secondly, we might think that introspection would allow for sure knowledge of grace. Aquinas disagrees. Yes, we have immediate and certain access to our own consciousness. But God transcends human cognitive capabilities. It is beyond the ability of the human mind to detect the special divine presence involved in grace. The third source of knowledge would come from our consciousness of our own motivational and cognitive states. As Augustine

said, we can have good evidence that we have received grace and perseverance. We may be conscious of delighting in God and rejecting worldly
things, and we may be sure that we have not committed any terrible sins.
These things would be signs that we have received grace. But still, we
could not know with absolute certainty.[30]

Regarding those to whom God gives grace, does He give it to all
equally? Aquinas says both "Yes" and "No". Sanctifying grace – the grace
to persevere to the end – leads one to God and eternal beatitude, and,
since the destination is the same for all, one could say that all receive
"equal" grace. But some are more brightly illumined by the light of grace
than others. Why is that? In part it is due to the extent of the human
agent's freely preparing himself to receive grace – but, of course, that
preparation itself is the result of divine grace, so the question remains.
A more fundamental answer is that diversity is important to the order
within the Church, as it is to the natural world. It is better to have the
inequality which contributes to the good of the whole.[31] In keeping with
the thought that the order within the Church requires diversity, Aquinas,
following St. Paul in First Corinthians (12: 8–10), enumerates various
gifts of grace. For example, there are gifts of grace that enable one to
preach, or to prophesy, or to interpret.[32] The Holy Spirit is very busy in
the human community bestowing grace to restore fallen human beings
and enable them to come to God and to cling to Him until death, thus
allowing them to arrive at the ultimate good of the beatific vision.

God, through grace, is actively achieving His plan for the world. But
this raises another hard question. If God is in the process of realizing His
plan for creation, wouldn't that mean He has foreknowledge of where
things are headed? Surely God does not have just an educated opinion
about what will happen. And doesn't His plan include a final, just judgment of humanity? Then it would seem that human beings must have free
will – a topic that has already come up several times. AAA all hold that
human agents make free choices. But (as Augustine sets out the dilemma)
if God knows today that I choose X tomorrow, when tomorrow comes
I cannot fail to choose X. It seems to be necessary that I choose X. And
don't necessity and freedom conflict? The next chapter will address the
question of how a commitment to divine foreknowledge can be reconciled with an equally strong commitment to human free will.

Notes

1 There are many different "graces", but we will focus on what AAA have to say
  about the grace that leads to salvation.
2 Augustine, *On Grace and Free Will* 20; Anselm, *On the Harmony of God's Foreknowledge, Predestination, and Grace with Free Choice (De concordia)* Book 3.3.

3 This is the official teaching of the Roman Catholic Church and of many Protestant churches.

4 *On Free Will.*

5 *On Nature and Grace* 2, *On the Grace of Christ and on Original Sin* Book 2.34. See also, Aquinas, *Summa theologiae* (ST) 1–2 Q. 109 art. 7.

6 *On Grace and Free Will* 15.

7 Augustine records issues from the tribunal in *On the Proceedings of Pelagius.*

8 *On the Grace of Christ and On Original Sin* Book 1.3.

9 *On the Grace of Christ and on Original Sin* Book 1.24 and following.

10 *On Nature and Grace* 8.

11 *On the Grace of Christ and on Free Will* Book 2.26 and 28 and 34.

12 *Against Two Letters of the Pelagians* Book 1.2.

13 Augustine, *On Grace and Free Will, On Rebuke and Grace* 6–7, 45; Aquinas, SCG Book 3.148, ST 1–2 Q. 109 art. 6 ad 1 and Q. 113 art. 3 and Q. 114 art. 9.

14 His *On Rebuke and Grace* attempts to respond to this problem.

15 *De concordia* Book 3.

16 *De concordia* Book 3.4.

17 *De concordia* Book 3.5.

18 SCG Book 3.147.

19 SCG Book 3.159–160.

20 Augustine, *On Grace and Free Will* 44–45, *Against Two Letters of the Pelagians* Book 4.16, *On Rebuke and Grace* 19; Anselm, *Proslogion* 10–11; Aquinas, SCG Book 4.161.

21 *On Grace and Free Will* 44.

22 *On the Virgin Conception and Original Sin* 23

23 "Limbo" is discussed in the Supplement to ST 3 Qs. 70–71.

24 *Catechism of the Catholic Church* 1261.

25 *On Grace and Free Will* 18.20.

26 Augustine, *On Rebuke and Grace* 10–17, *On the Predestination of the Saints,* Book 2, *On Perseverance;* Aquinas, ST 1–2 Q.109 art. 10.

27 *On Rebuke and Grace* 49.

28 *On Man's Perfection in Righteousness* 10.

29 *On Rebuke and Grace* Chapter 40. Is there a dilemma here? If one *knows* with certainty that one is among the elect, then one is among the elect. So it would seem that one could not come to be so full of pride as to fail to reach heaven.

30 ST 1–2 Q. 112 art. 5.

31 ST 1–2 Q.112 art. 4.

32 SCG Book 4.154.

5

DIVINE FOREKNOWLEDGE AND HUMAN FREE WILL

Introduction

One of the perennial questions in the philosophy of religion is this: Is it possible to reconcile the claim that God has knowledge of future events with the claim that human beings have free will? The problem, as Augustine spells out in Book 3 of his *On Free Will*, is that if God knows today what you are going to choose tomorrow it is impossible that you should choose anything other than what God knows that you will choose. (I focus on *choosing* rather than on doing some overt deed since, if there is human free will, it is manifested in making free choices. AAA are especially concerned with the character of the agent and so they hold that the moral value of an overt deed derives from the moral value attached to the agent's process of choosing to do it.) God is omniscient, so He knows all there is to know, and if He knows that something is the case, then it is the case. And there is no changing the past. When tomorrow gets to be today, you cannot possibly change what God knew yesterday. But doesn't this mean that, when it comes time for you to choose, you don't really have any option but to choose what God foreknew you would choose? But if you *must* choose what God foreknew, then it seems to be the case that your choice is a matter of necessity. And choices made by necessity are not free. So apparently there is a conflict between God having foreknowledge of all future events and human beings have free will.

We will look at why AAA take it to be vital to embrace both divine foreknowledge and human free will, and then we will address the problem by looking at how the history of an answer develops from Augustine to Anselm. This history will include Boethius (480–524 CE) who builds on Augustine's work and prefigures important points in both Anselm's and Aquinas's responses to the apparent conflict between freedom and foreknowledge. Anselm's solution is powerful because it allows for a reconciliation of divine foreknowledge with human freedom even on a libertarian

DOI: 10.4324/9781003202080-6

account of human free will. Finally, we will look at Aquinas' position briefly. The texts where he attempts to reconcile freedom and foreknowledge are confusing in that some suggest a view similar to Anselm's, while others are rooted in Aquinas's compatibilist understanding of freedom. The two approaches are not contradictory, though, and Aquinas may simply have embraced both.

The Importance of Both Human Freedom and Divine Foreknowledge

One way some philosophers, past and present, have "solved" the apparent conflict is by rejecting either divine foreknowledge or human free will. AAA cannot adopt this "solution" since they hold that both foreknowledge and freedom are crucial to a Christian picture of the universe. There are several ways of arguing that God must know the future. Simply pointing out that God is omniscient won't fully defend divine foreknowledge, though. This is because it could be argued that omniscience entails knowing all there is to know, but the future is not there to be known. Thus even an omniscient being cannot know the future. (This way of denying divine foreknowledge was condemned in the thirteenth century by the Bishop of Paris, Etienne Tempier, in the *Condemnation of 1277* #15.[1]) Anselm adopts a somewhat different approach. God is that than which no greater can be conceived. A being that knows all things is a greater being than one that does not, and so we ought to say that God knows the future. If it could be *proven* that knowledge of the future is simply impossible, even for the perfect and unlimited source of all, then this argument would not work. But the burden of proof is on the one who insists that the future cannot be known. There does not seem to be anything logically contradictory or unthinkable about someone knowing the future. The thesis is often portrayed more or less coherently in time travel stories. And, as we will see, Anselm and Aquinas offer a picture of the relationship of time to divine eternity which addresses the question of *how* God might be able to know the future. (Augustine presents a long and thoughtful meditation on the nature of time in *Confessions* Book 11, but scholars debate what his conclusions are.) So, absent a powerful proof that the future cannot be known by anyone, divine omniscience must include knowledge of the future.

A similar argument starts with the general monotheist claim that God is omnipotent. Assuming foreknowledge is *possible*, a being who foreknows the future has a wider scope of action than a being who does not. If God is that than which no greater can be conceived, He must be able to do everything logically possible for a perfect and unlimited being to do, and knowledge of the future supports that understanding of omnipotence. Looking at divine power from a more specifically Christian angle, AAA assume that God is the "Sovereign" of the universe. He has a care for humanity, guiding and ruling us both on the species, and on the individual, level. Divine sovereignty entails divine foreknowledge. If God is in charge and has a plan that He is bringing about for the universe, then He cannot be ignorant of the future. He must know that His plan will be realized. This is especially important in connection with one way AAA deal with the problem of evil. Why does God permit evil? Because He is going to bring good out of it. This answer works much better if we take it that God is *sure* that He will use the evil to produce some future good than if we think that He is hopeful, or *almost* sure, or strongly believes, or has an educated opinion, that the future good will come about.

There seems to be a great deal of scriptural support for the idea that God knows the future. The Nicene Creed includes the claim that God's incarnation as Jesus Christ was foretold by the prophets. As Christians read the Old Testament, God told the prophets that the Savior would come long before the birth of Christ. To take another scriptural example; shortly before Jesus is captured to be sent to His death, He tells Peter that Peter will betray Him three times before the cock crows twice. This is an especially interesting example of divine foreknowledge since the event foreknown seems clearly to be a free choice made by Peter. There are many more examples of what look to be instances of divine foreknowledge in Scripture, and so AAA will insist, on both philosophical and scriptural grounds, that God knows the future.

Regarding free will, we have seen in the earlier chapters of this book – especially Chapter Two on original sin – that AAA all maintain the importance of human freedom. They propose somewhat different theories of free will, but all agree that we human beings are a very valuable kind thing not just because we are rational, but also because we are free. Everything that exists is good, but human beings are especially made in the image of God as rational and free. We can be morally responsible for our choices and deeds. Even outside of a theological context, most philosophers hold that human agents must be free, on some understanding of freedom, if they are to bear moral responsibility and be deserving of praise and blame. AAA all believe, based on good scriptural authority, that God will judge humanity justly for the good and evil that we have done. We must be free to bear moral responsibility and so be appropriate subjects for that judgment.

Moreover, Anselm, because he adopts a libertarian analysis of human free will, can make a powerful move in addressing the problem of moral evil. Moral evil (as we are using the term) refers to the wickedness of created agents and the bad consequences of that wickedness. Why would God allow it? Anselm can appeal to a version of what is today called the "Free Will Defense". One reason that God allows human beings (and angels) to sin is that our ability to *choose* to be good requires morally significant options, and that entails the real possibility that we will choose badly.[2] God could prevent us from ever sinning, but that would require removing our ability to ever *choose* rightly. It would require removing our free will. Free will is such a great good that God leaves us free despite the moral evil we cause.[3] For Anselm holding that human agents are free helps deal with moral evil. AAA all paint a picture of our God-created universe in which both human free will and divine foreknowledge are necessary elements. How can the two be reconciled?

The Development of an Answer from Augustine to Anselm[4]

It is Augustine who first attempts to resolve the problem in detail in a Christian context. His statement of the apparent conflict was set out briefly above, but to facilitate the discussion we can spell it out again here in numbered premises:

1 God knows today (time T) that some agent (S) will choose X tomorrow (T+1). [Let X stand for some action the agent is considering or some object the agent wishes to pursue.]
2 God cannot be mistaken.
3 [So when tomorrow comes S cannot possibly fail to choose X.] S chooses X as a matter of necessity.
4 But choices made by necessity are not free.

Conclusion: Therefore free will and divine foreknowledge conflict.

Augustine writes his *On Free Will* in the form of a dialogue and his style is somewhat meditative. He makes a number of interesting points about free will in his winding discussion, but the core of his explanation for why the above argument fails can be outlined in a straightforward way. Augustine notes that the apparent conflict arises even if we substitute some other knower for God in Premise 1. We can call this new knower K and rewrite Premise 1 as follows:

1 K knows today that S chooses X tomorrow.

If we make this substitution, Premises 3 and 4 remain the same. This is because, at least for philosophers, the definition of "knowledge" entails that what is known is true.[5] So if *anyone* knows today that S chooses X tomorrow, S cannot possibly fail to choose X tomorrow. Premise 2 is not actually doing any work in the argument. We can get rid of it. Premise 3 still follows, since there is a kind of necessity involved in S's choice of X. However, it is not the sort of causal necessity that undermines free will. It is the logical necessity that follows from the definition of knowledge. "If K knows X, then X." Anyone's knowledge entails that what is known to be the case, is the case. But mere knowledge does not exercise any causal *determination*, that is causally efficacious "force" to bring about what is the case. Premise 4, that a choice made "by necessity" is not free, is true as long as "necessity" in this premise is understood to be the sort of causal power that would determine or compel a choice for this or that and hence render it unfree. (If you are tied to a chair then "necessarily" you remain in the chair. You are compelled to do so.) Each premise in the argument may be true, depending on how one understands the various terms. But the whole argument fails because the meaning of "necessity" which would make Premise 3 true is different from the meaning which would make Premise 4 true. The use of the term "necessity" is equivocal. If "necessity" in Premise 4 just meant the logical necessity of "If K knows that X, then X" then Premise 4 would be false. The logical necessity entailed by a fact being known does not entail the necessity that conflicts with free will.

Augustine has succeeded in showing the failure of the argument for a conflict between freedom and foreknowledge as he had set it out. But this is only the first step in a solution to the problem. Boethius, in the early sixth century, adds an important link to the chain of reasoning that will lead, centuries later, to Anselm's powerful solution. Boethius is best known for his *Consolation of Philosophy,* a widely read work that asks the question, "Why does God let bad things happen to good people?" Boethius repeats the Augustinian explanation that foreknowledge indeed involves a logical necessity – If God knows today that S will choose X tomorrow, S cannot possibly fail to choose X tomorrow. But this sort of necessity does not conflict with free will. Boethius labels it a "conditional" necessity: on the condition that X is known, necessarily X is the case. Boethius agrees that the argument for the conflict between freedom and foreknowledge as Augustine stated it is fallacious. Nevertheless, he points out that a thorny question has not been answered: *How* does God foreknow free choices?

Boethius allows that even *human beings* can have knowledge of future events. We can know, he thinks, that the sun will rise tomorrow. But this foreknowledge must be based on our knowledge of things or events which we can observe in the present and which will necessitate those future events – "necessitate" in the sense of causally *determining* them in a way that rules out voluntary action. From the human perspective, only non-freely occurring events can be foreknown. We can know that the sun will rise tomorrow because the sun does what it does through natural necessity. The causal powers at work in the laws of nature determine the rising of the sun. So, says Boethius, let us grant that God's *knowledge* does not necessitate future choices in a way that would render them unfree. Still, must it not be the case that God can foreknow future choices only because they are causally necessitated by present events and hence are not free?[6] (This suggestion is also condemned by Bishop Tempier in #15 of the *Condemnation of 1277*.)

No, says Boethius. This argument fails to appreciate that the divine perspective is very different from the human perspective. Unlike temporally limited creatures who live in time, God lives in eternity. Boethius introduces a famous definition of eternity, which Aquinas will quote later, "Eternity, then, is the whole, simultaneous and perfect possession of boundless life...[It] must hold as present the infinity of moving time". God sees all events as if they were present, as if He were looking down on them all from the highest peak of the world. He does not need to deduce future events from their causes in the present.[7] Boethius takes an important step by invoking divine eternity in responding to the problem of freedom and foreknowledge. Augustine, in a number of places, offers insightful and influential thoughts on the nature of time, the nature of divine eternity, and the relationship of the eternal God to our changing world.[8] But Augustine does not appeal to divine eternity in dealing with the dilemma of freedom and foreknowledge. It is Boethius who adds this crucial piece to the puzzle.

However there are questions to be asked about Boethius's attempted solution. How, exactly, does he see the relationship between time and eternity? And how, exactly, is it that God, in His eternity, knows future choices? Boethius, in the *Consolation* at a point well before his introduction of divine eternity, has raised a worry. He says that it is absurd that God's knowledge could be produced by our choices.[9] God is the absolute source of all and we certainly cannot "teach" Him anything. Having explained that God knows our future choices from His unique perspective in eternity, Boethius goes on to say that God knows our future choices because He knows what He Himself will cause.[10] (This proposal, too, is condemned by Bishop Tempier in the *Condemnation of 1277* #15. The Bishop seems to have had libertarian leanings.) Boethius's understanding of the relationship of time and eternity is not clear. God knows events in time because He causes them and, "as if" they were present. But the events themselves may be in the future, even for God.

Many philosophers agree with Boethius that, even though God causes human choices, human agents can be free in a way that grounds moral responsibility. In earlier chapters, especially Chapter Two on original sin, I spelled out this compatibilist analysis of free will and attributed it to Augustine and Aquinas. It is certainly Augustine's position when he is opposing the Pelagians as discussed in Chapter Four on Grace. And Aquinas is clear that God is the cause of all things. The act of choosing is a sort of thing, and so God causes it. God causes our choices, even the choice to sin, as the primary cause (the cause that makes things exist ex nihilo). We have to say this, according to Augustine and Aquinas, since otherwise we undermine divine omnipotence. Nonetheless, we willingly cause our choices as secondary causes, and so we can be justly judged. Augustine and Aquinas could both accept Boethius's explanation for how God knows the future; He knows what He is going to cause. But Augustine never makes this point explicitly. Aquinas does propose this solution and develop it more fully than did Boethius.

Boethius's explanation for how God knows future choices did not satisfy everyone. Many people share the intuition that if God were the ultimate cause of our choices, it would be unfair for Him to judge us and especially unfair to punish us. The debate over how to reconcile divine foreknowledge with human freedom simmered on in Western Europe after Boethius's attempt in the sixth century. It got ugly in the ninth century, producing a lot of rancorous debate.[11] It is Anselm, at the end of the eleventh and beginning of the twelfth century, who really advances the discussion. He builds on Augustine's point about conditional necessity and Boethius's claim that God knows "in eternity". But he goes further than his predecessors by addressing the roots of the problem, spelling out in detail how created agency works and how God's eternal knowledge is related to temporal events. I noted in Chapter Two that, as I read him, Anselm defends a "libertarian" position on free will. In order to be free in a way that allows for moral responsibility, and to be praiseworthy and blameworthy, the created agent must confront genuinely open options and choose *a se*, from himself. It must be "up to" the created agent to opt for good or evil. Anselm rejects the claim that God must cause every event including human choices. Anselm proposes that God is the cause of everything with ontological status, but that created choices are not "things" which add to the being of what exists in the universe. God is omnipotent, the source of all existents, but human agents are responsible for their choices. God is the cause of everything that exists, but not of everything that happens.

But doesn't insisting on a libertarian account of free will make the problem of reconciling free will with divine foreknowledge worse? Anselm's understanding of created free will, which holds that the created agent chooses *a se,* entails the "grounding principle"; the truth about a free choice is "grounded" in (based on, derived from) the fact of that free choice itself. Hence knowledge of the choice depends on the agent's actually making the choice. If God knows today that S chooses X tomorrow this must be because God has access to S choosing X tomorrow. To explain how that can be Anselm proposes a theory of time and eternity that is suggested by both Augustine and Boethius, but not clearly spelled out by either of them.

Anselm's theory of time and eternity is explained most fully in his last finished philosophical work, *On the Harmony of the Foreknowledge, the Predestination, and the Grace of God with Free Choice (De concordia).* In this work, he explicitly addresses the problem of reconciling free will and divine foreknowledge. But he has begun to develop important foundations of his argument in earlier work, especially in his *Proslogion.* Created free will is not a topic in this work, but the nature of divine eternity and the relationship of the eternal to our temporal world is. On the nature of time, I understand Anselm to subscribe to "isotemporalism".[12] (He may be the first to propose this view.) All times – what to some temporal perceiver at some time are past, present, and future – exist equally. Before and after are objectively real, but past, present, and future are subjective to a given perceiver at a given time.[13] Time must be isotemporal because God – whose power and knowledge are the source of all reality – "contains" all times.[14] This follows upon Anselm's description of God as that than which no greater can be conceived. A being that can know and act upon all times is greater than one who is circumscribed by existing only at each time and whose life cannot be simple (that is, perfectly unified) because it is spread out across all the moments of time.[15]

The clearest proof text for Anselm's isotemporalism is in *De concordia* (1.5). Here he writes, "Just as the present time contains all place and whatever is in any place, in the same way the eternal present encloses all time and whatever exists in any time...For eternity has its own unique simultaneity in which exist all the things which exist at the same place or time, and whatever exists in the different places and times." All the times actually exist, since Anselm draws a parallel between time and place. It cannot be that only some places are "here" to God and others just do not exist. So with time, it cannot be that there is a discrete "now" for God such that other times are gone or yet to come. All times are present to divine eternity. And since God's eternal act of knowing is the cause of all that is, if God sees all times as equally "there" in reality, then all times really are "there" in reality – that is isotemporalism.

In *De concordia* Anselm follows Augustine and Boethius on the point about conditional necessity: Yes, there is a necessity entailed by divine foreknowledge, but it is the conditional necessity of "Necessarily, if X is known, then X". Anselm also invokes divine eternity to help deal with *how* God can know the future. But unlike Boethius, Anselm is clear that all events are immediately present to God. God knows eternally what S chooses at any time, because all times, and all the events they contain, are immediately present to God. This move fits with libertarianism and conforms to the grounding principle; God knows that S chooses X at T *because* S chooses X at T. Explicitly embracing isotemporalism allows Anselm to propose a plausible way to reconcile divine foreknowledge with libertarian free will.

Anselm still has the worry that he could seem to be saying that our choices "impact" God, and this is problematic since Anselm, like Augustine and Aquinas, holds that creatures cannot exercise any causal power over God. But, to offer a tentative suggestion, perhaps Anselm could appeal to his analysis of the process of choice which holds that our choice consists of our pursuing one God-given desire over another to the point where one becomes the intention and the other ceases to be viable. He might argue that God knows what we choose because He knows which of the conflicting, God-given motives He Himself is keeping in being past the point of choice. It is true that if S had not chosen X, God would not know that S chooses X, but it does not follow that S's choice exerts any sort of causal force or power over God. And note that, given a libertarian analysis of free will, this problem associated with God knowing that S chooses X *because* S chooses X would arise even if God existed in time and so could not "fore"know that S chooses X, but could only know it by observing it in the present. On libertarianism the truth about a free choice is rooted in the fact of the agent actually making the choice, and the same point holds for God's knowledge of the choice whether God's knowledge is eternal or temporal.

Aquinas on Freedom and Foreknowledge

Aquinas's solution to the foreknowledge and free will problem is difficult to pin down because various things he says seem to point in different directions. Aquinas quotes Boethius's definition of eternity as "…the whole, simultaneous and perfect possession of boundless life."[16] I noted above that Aquinas, as a compatibilist on free will, could follow Boethius in saying that God knows the future choices of created agents because He is going to cause those choices. And in several places he says roughly that: God can know future things like the artisan who can know what he hasn't made yet.[17] God knows Himself as the cause and therefore He can know the effects before they exist.[18] But Boethius's text leaves it open whether or not God sees the future "as if" it were present to Him or because it *actually is* present to Him. To explain God in eternity seeing all times Boethius appeals to the analogy of someone seeing things spread out below him as if he occupied the highest peak. Nevertheless, the analogy does not settle the question of whether what God sees is actually existent or is seen "as if" it were.

Though Aquinas does not subscribe to Anselm's libertarian picture of free will, he often seems to agree with the earlier philosopher that God knows (what are to us) future things and events because they are present to Him. He writes that God's eternity includes all times.[19] He explains that, concerning things that do not exist because they were in the past or will be in the future, God has "knowledge of vision". That is, He sees all times and what is in time as present to Him.[20] This text is confusing. If we take it to mean that all times are actually present to God, that would seem to entail that all times and all the various things that exist at all the times of the universe are equally real. All times and what they contain are "there" in the spatio-temporal universe. That is isotemporalism. But Aquinas is explaining how God can know things that *do not exist* because they are past or future. The isotemporalist can say that times that are past or future relative to some temporal perceiver at a given time do not exist *at that time*. But he cannot say that they do not exist simpliciter. Aquinas expresses no qualification regarding the non-existence of the past and future. He goes on to say that God knows contingent things simultaneously because divine eternity comprises all time.[21] This, again, sounds like isotemporalism. And he offers an analogy similar to Boethius's but more fully developed. Imagine people traveling along a road. They cannot see the people coming along the road behind them. But someone surveying the whole road from a great height can see all the people traveling along the road.[22] Since all the people on the road exist equally, this analogy suggests isotemporalism. All times exist equally so that God can see them all from His "height" in eternity. But where he is discussing divine creation he makes a claim that seems to conflict with isotemporalism. He says that all place was created simultaneously since place is permanent, but time, not being permanent, was created only in its beginning, "just as nothing is held in the action of time except the "now".[23] This suggests that, in the beginning, only a discreet moment of time existed and that the "now" is unique, claims that conflict with isotemporalism. Aquinas certainly believes that divine foreknowledge and human freedom can be reconciled, but the textual evidence from his two major works for how this reconciliation is to be understood is puzzling. If he is an isotemporalist then he holds that God sees all times as immediately present to Him because all times actually exist equally. But even if he is not an isotemporalist, he certainly says that God is the cause of all that happens and so God can know all human choices at all times because He is the cause of them all.

One reason it is so important to maintain both human free will and divine foreknowledge is that the Christian is told to hope for eternal beatitude with God in heaven – a future destiny flowing from present free behavior. The Christian picture of the afterlife involves a number of issues. AAA take it that the human person is a psycho-physical unity of body and soul. What happens to the soul when the body dies? And – even more problematic – what happens to the body? AAA all accept the traditional Christian claim that the body will be resurrected, so the human being will experience an embodied afterlife. How can that be? In the next chapter we will see how Augustine and Aquinas address these issues. (Sadly for philosophers, Anselm died before he was able to write the work he intended on these questions.)

Notes

1 Being thus condemned does not entail being permanently rejected by the Church. Several of Aquinas's views were condemned in the *Condemnation of 1277*. The condemnations were lifted after he was canonized.
2 *On the Fall of the Devil* 13 and 14.
3 As discussed in Chapter Two, I read both Augustine and Aquinas as compatibilists who hold that we are free agents even though God causes our choices. On this understanding of free will, God could make it the case that human beings always *freely* refrain from sinning, so they cannot propose the Free Will Defense to help explain why God permits moral evil. Some scholars find something like the Free Will Defense in Book 2 of Augustine's *On Free Will*. Here he does say that the human will is free and it is a good thing because without it we could not choose well. But he never says that the open option to choose evil is necessary for us to be free to choose the good.
4 Some of this section quotes or closely follows my "Freedom and Foreknowledge: A Case Study in Progress in Theology" presented at the Progress in Theology Winter Seminar at the Abraham Kuyper Center, Vrije Universiteit in Amsterdam, January 2022.
5 Different philosophers define "knowledge" differently, but that it requires the truth of what is known is standard. One way Augustine defines "knowledge" is roughly "true belief acquired through immediate access to the known."
6 *Consolation* Book 5. Prose 4.
7 *Consolation* Book 5. Prose 6
8 Book 11 of the *Confessions* is his most well-known text on time and eternity. There is also an interesting discussion in his *On the Literal Meaning of Genesis* Book 4 where he is wrestling with how to understand the "days" in *Genesis*.
9 *Consolation* Book 5. Prose 3
10 *Consolation* Book 5. Prose 6.
11 It also produced an acute and provocative work called *On Predestination* by John Scottus Eriugena (c.800-c.877 CE).
12 The position is sometimes called "four-dimensionalism", based on the thought that physical things exist in three spatial dimensions but also in time, a fourth

dimension. That is not the best term for two reasons: first, there could be worlds in which objects exist in more spatial dimensions, and second, there could be non-spatial things – angels for example – which are citizens of our temporal universe, but which do not exist in four dimensions. The other common name is "eternalism", but this is confusing since it could suggest the mistaken view that the universe is eternal in the same way that God is.

13 This view of time is assumed in most time travel stories. If someone can travel from what is their present to their past or future, what is to them past and future must exist. And once the time traveler gets to past or future, that time becomes their present.

14 *Proslogion* 19

15 God must be simple since a being composed of parts is in some way dependent on those parts. Moreover, a being composed of parts can be "decomposed", if only in the intellect. But that than which no greater can be thought cannot even be thought to be pulled apart. *Proslogion* 18

16 *Summa theologiae* (ST) 1 Q. 10 art. 1.

17 *Summa contra gentiles* (SCG) Book 1.66. 3.

18 SCG Book 1.66.6. See also 67.7 and 68.3 and 8.

19 ST 1 Q. 10 art. 2 ad 4.

20 ST 1 Q. 14 art. 9.

21 ST 1 Q. 14 art. 13.

22 ST 1 Q. 14 art. 13 ad 3.

23 ST 1 Q. 66 art. 4 ad 5. My translation is not elegant. The Latin is "…sicut etiam modo nihil est accipere in actu de tempore nisi nunc."

6

THE AFTERLIFE

Introduction

The goal of the Christian life, as far as Augustine, Anselm, and Aquinas are concerned, is perfect, everlasting happiness in the presence of God. Nothing could be better than that. But is this goal too good to be true? Is it mere wishful thinking? In the course of this work we have focused mainly on doctrines that the Christian accepts on faith – like the Trinity and the Incarnation – taking them as given, and then trying to gain a deeper understanding of what they mean. One might suppose that the claim that human individuals experience an immortal afterlife would be a doctrine that could be accepted only as a matter of faith. But AAA do not see it that way. There are many interconnected premises involved in discussion of the afterlife, and many have been the subjects of philosophical investigation, even outside of Christian circles. Both Augustine and Aquinas draw heavily on non-Christian philosophers in their analysis of the afterlife. (We must largely set aside Anselm, since he died before he could write his intended treatise on the soul. I will argue at the end of the chapter, though, that of the three, it is Anselm who has the theoretical resources to provide an adequate account of damnation.)

That human individuals have immaterial, immortal souls was accepted on philosophical grounds by many non-Christian thinkers. That there is some manner of heaven was a widely embraced view which, given a few starting assumptions, can be philosophically demonstrated. Even the Christian doctrine that the body will be resurrected and reunited with the soul can find some philosophical support, although it is a view that many non-Christian philosophers (and even some early Christian intellectuals!) found incoherent and unwholesome. In the present chapter we will intertwine analysis of various aspects related to the afterlife with philosophical attempts to prove key elements in the traditional Christian picture. First we will review a simple, standard argument for the existence of heaven.

DOI: 10.4324/9781003202080-7

Next we will address the nature of the human person. On AAA's understanding, body and soul together constitute the human individual. But why should we think we have souls? And why think they are immortal? More troubling – at least for AAA – is the view that the body joins the soul in immortality. Yet the claim is inescapable from the perspective of Scripture and is not incoherent. Then we will look at some attempts, especially by Aquinas, to describe the afterlife of the blessed in heaven. We will conclude the chapter with a look at the unhappy topic of hell.

The "proof" for heaven is quite simple. (One finds it spelled out in the work of Anselm and Aquinas, and Augustine suggests it in various places.)[1] It requires only a few premises. First, our universe, including all the people in it, was made by a good, omnipotent God. Second, human beings were created by God with a desire for happiness. This desire does not entail limitation. We never think of saying, "I've had enough happiness. Now I want to be miserable for a while". We want thorough, continuous, unending happiness. We want it, but we cannot get it in this life, as Augustine and Aquinas point out.[2] Whatever happiness we enjoy in this present existence is fleeting and is always marred by that lurking darkness in the background, the fear of death. But God would not have created in us a desire that cannot be satisfied. It must be possible, then, for human beings to enjoy the desired, unending beatitude (happiness) on the other side of death. Heaven is at least a possibility, and the theological virtue of hope is grounded deep in human nature.

The Nature of the Human Person

The Christian tradition, exemplified by Augustine and Aquinas, holds that the human person is a unity of body and soul. There is the physical part of us, available to the senses, the body. And there is the soul, the part of the person that enables him to reason. For AAA the soul is more than what we today call the "mind". In classical thought all living things have souls. The soul is what animates, gives life to, the living thing. What is special about human souls is that they can reason, so it is legitimate for our purposes to understand the soul as the thinking part.[3] (For Aquinas this may be a poor way to phrase the claim. It is the *person* who reasons, not a "part" of the person. More on this below.) That the human person is not simply the physical, observable body or simply the conscious thinking part, the soul, but rather a combination of the two may seem rather obvious. Outside of the philosophical community one does not often run into people who deny either that they have bodies or that they are sometimes thinking. However, contemporary intellectuals often disagree with this assessment of the human person as a unified being composed of body and soul. The disagreement can take two forms which, prima facie, look to be in tension, but often it is one and the same contemporary intellectual propounding both arguments. One form involves the claim that the human being is no more than body. This view is called "materialism" or "physicalism" and is often rooted in the broader assumption that all that exists is material or physical. We will look below at reasons Augustine and Aquinas give for supposing that humans must have souls as well as bodies. A standard, contemporary response to physicalism is to point to the so-called "problem of consciousness": It does not seem possible to analyze mental phenomena as physical phenomena. Say that you are looking at a painting of Napoleon. You are experiencing an image of Napoleon. Perhaps your image of Napoleon, as you are considering the painting, is closely, even *very* closely, associated with particular brain activity. But we will not be able to observe the image of Napoleon you are experiencing, no matter how minutely we examine your brain. One way to put the point is to note that mental phenomena, like your image of Napoleon, are absolutely private to you, while the activity going on in your brain is, in principle, public. If we had the right instruments we could observe your brain at work. The motivation for insisting that the human person is simply body is often the desire to fit everything under the umbrella of the hard sciences, which operate by observation and quantification. So denying soul is "scientific". It is also argued that it is more parsimonious – simpler – to posit that the human person is one sort of thing, body. Both of these motivations were known, in earlier incarnations, to Augustine and Aquinas.[4] Neither was impressed by (what they would take to be) a misguided "scientism". And, while it is good to be "parsimonious" when explaining things, it is important that your theory is not *so* simple that it cannot explain what needs explaining. As we will see, Augustine and Aquinas both hold that the fact of human rationality requires a soul.

An alternative way of rejecting the thought that the human person is soul and body is to insist that the *real* you is just your soul. You are to be identified with the thinking part. Your body is rather like your car. You may be "in" it right now, but it is not really *you*. You become one of us, a true human person, when you are able to think self-reflectively, that is you can "step back" and recognize yourself as a thinking, feeling, desiring being over time. Thus, many contemporary philosophers hold that fetuses and infants are not human persons. Yes, they have human bodies that develop continuously until adulthood, but they are not real members of the human community until they can think in a fairly sophisticated fashion. And someone who loses the ability to think self-reflectively is no longer present as a person. Many contemporary utilitarians (philosophers who hold that the intrinsic good is happiness or the satisfaction of preferences or something similar) are materialists regarding what there is in the universe, and yet they hold that one is not a human person unless one can be self-reflective enough to have desires about one's future. They illustrate my point that sometimes it is the same intellectual who says that the human person is only body and also that the human person is really the thinking part.[5]

The view that the human person is simply, or really, just their soul was very popular in Augustine's day. Plato had propounded the thought centuries earlier, and he continued to have many followers. On Plato's account, you are your soul. Your soul is immortal. It existed before it joined your present body and will continue to exist after this present body dies. Through all eternity it is reincarnated in new bodies. Sometimes Plato even suggests that your soul might go into a lower animal. Your body is a sort of prison for your soul. Being joined to a body makes you forget the wonderful truths you knew previously in a disembodied state, and it hinders you in pursuing wisdom due to the distractions which your senses and bodily desires throw in your path.[6] In Augustine's day even many Christian intellectuals were taken with this very "spiritual" assessment of human nature. Augustine, though, is adamant that the Christian has to reject this approach. The Second Person of the Trinity, the Son, became man, and part of what that involved was taking on a human body. As I noted in the chapter on the Incarnation, in the early Church there were many intellectuals who tried to avoid this conclusion. Inspired by Platonism and a host of related world views they hoped to shield God from involvement with that gross matter. Augustine insists that Scripture and Church teaching are clear; God became a true human being, and that meant assuming a human soul and a human body. That is the position ratified by the Council of Chalcedon shortly after Augustine's death. Christians have no justification for denigrating the body. True, the body with its distractions can be difficult to deal with, as Plato said. But the problem is not with the divinely created body per se. The problem is with the disorder introduced into the human person by sin.[7] From Augustine's day to ours the Church has insisted, against those who would argue to the contrary, that the human person is body and soul combined.

Though Augustine and Aquinas both hold that the human person is a unity of soul and body, their understanding of what that means is somewhat different. Augustine, agreeing with Plato to some extent, takes soul and body to be two, different things. They can exist separately, as at death. Your soul can survive the death of your body because it is of a different, and immortal, nature. Your disembodied soul after death is truly *you* but leading an incomplete human existence until it receives its body back at the resurrection. Aquinas embraces a more Aristotelian approach. It is a more complex and difficult position over which there is much debate, and we will spell it out just enough to motivate the further discussion in this chapter.

According to Aristotle, all physical things are composed of matter and form, that is, they are "hylomorphic" (from the Greek words for matter and form). The form endows a thing with its existence and its nature. The matter "individuates", that is, it allows for many different things to have the same form. So we might say of a horse, that it has the form of horseness and it is discrete from other individual horses because of the matter going to make up this particular horse. The form of a living thing is the animating, "life-giving", principle in the thing, and so the form of a living thing can be called its "soul". The human soul is the form of the human being, and it is unique among other animal souls in that it is rational. In general, for Aristotle, form and matter exist together in a thing, such that it would make no sense to posit either of them existing in separation. You don't have the beach ball's spherical form over here and its plastic matter over there. But in his book *On the Soul* Aristotle suggests that human knowledge requires some separation of the thinking part from the rest of the human being. He discusses this in a passage that has troubled commentators from Aristotle's day to ours.[8] One possible reading, adopted by some of Aquinas's Islamic predecessors, would hold that all of humanity shares one thinking mind! Aquinas adamantly opposes that position. But he does argue that the rational, human soul, because its primary job is to understand, engages in activity that is not inevitably tied to the body. Understanding here means something like thinking theoretically. Doing science. Being able to both ask and answer the question, "What is this?" Lower animals may be able to process and remember quite a bit of information, but they do not step back and wonder what things are. For Aquinas our natural cognitive processes begin with sense observation, and so the body, with its different senses, is crucial for us to amass knowledge. But the senses can give us only images of individual, corporeal things. A collection of images from the senses does not enable us to answer the "What is it?" question. For that we need to grasp the form that makes this individual to be the kind of thing it is. Our intellects are capable of operating on the data from the senses to allow us to understand the forms of things. And, in Aquinas's view, this activity of the rational soul is not something the body is doing. The human soul, then, is unlike the souls of lower animals. Its primary job is not a bodily activity, and so it can survive separation from the body at death.

Aquinas's hylomorphism concerning the human person generates an interesting puzzle concerning the afterlife. It is a puzzle for historians trying to discern exactly what Aquinas's views were, and it is a puzzle for contemporary Thomists – followers of St. Thomas's philosophy – trying to figure out what the most philosophically and theologically adequate position is. The problem is this: If the human person is hylomorphic, then a person's body is not the person, but only part of the person. And a person's soul is not the person, but only part of the person. But then, one could argue that upon death, neither the dead body nor the surviving soul is the person. But then the person does not exist after death. Church tradition teaches that our bodies will be resurrected someday, so the soul will be reunited with its body, but what about that disembodied soul in the meantime? Tradition teaches that the soul will be judged immediately upon death and assigned to heaven (perhaps by way of purgatory) or hell. But that hardly seems fair, if we suppose it is the acts of the *person* that constitute the evidence for judgment. Augustine takes it that your soul really is you, even while it is cut off from your body. It is natural for human souls to be connected to bodies, and the soul desires to be reunited with the body, but that soul after death is still you, albeit incompletely. Some scholars attribute something like this view to Aquinas. It is labeled "survivalism", since the thought is that the human person does survive death as the soul. The main alternative is "corruptionism"; the human person ceases to exist at the separation of soul and body but comes into being again when the two are reunited at the resurrection of the body. An advantage of corruptionism is that it underscores how closely knit soul and body are on Aquinas's hylomorphic theory. Survivalism, however, seems more consonant with many traditional beliefs and practices concerning the afterlife. For example, in the tradition of Augustine and Aquinas we pray for the saints to intercede with God for us. We do not pray for the souls of the saints to intercede, but for the saints themselves to do so. It would take us too far afield to try to weigh in on this ongoing debate. I will write as if Aquinas is a survivalist, but the reader should note that the issue is far from settled.

Proofs for the Non-corporeal Soul and Its Immortality

The human soul gives life to the human being and is where the person's thinking occurs. If we think of the soul simply as a "life and consciousness" principle, then few humans will deny that they think and live. So in that minimal sense there is agreement that a soul exists. But to support the Christian picture of the afterlife, the soul must not be an aspect or part of the body. It must be separable from the body, and it must be capable of immortality. These are claims that one could believe on faith, but both Augustine and Aquinas offer reasons for accepting the incorporeal nature of the soul and the possibility (or necessity) of its immortality. We will look briefly at a few of their arguments.

Augustine proposes several different arguments to show that the soul is not corporeal. The contemporary philosopher is likely to find his arguments insufficiently developed, even in the original text, and here we can offer just a quick sketch to show what sort of arguments Augustine presents. Augustine himself is writing within a philosophical milieu in which the basic arguments he gives are well known. One argument begins with the very definition of "body". Bodies are spatially extended. A larger body occupies a larger space, and a smaller body occupies a smaller space. But soul is not like that. The whole soul is equally present to each and every part of the body. How do we know? Well, prick the smallest part of your body with a pin, and immediately *you* are aware, that is, your whole soul is aware, of that tiny prick. So your soul is not a corporeal thing contained in any part of the body, nor is it a physical substance diffused throughout your body, as if there were more soul in your leg and less in your toe.[9] Moreover, it is the nature of matter that one corporeal thing can become some other corporeal thing. You eat the carrot and some of that carrot becomes your flesh. And some of your flesh may become soil, and some of that soil may make up a part of a plant and on and on. We can trace this process of change among bodies, but we never find body changed into soul, nor soul into body. Soul, then, cannot be just a kind of body.[10]

Further, soul is capable of contemplating incorporeal objects. We can think about abstract objects, like mathematical equations. Such objects cannot exist as part of body.[11] This is reminiscent of the point made above about the problem of consciousness. Think hard about $7 + 3 = 10$. And let us grant, to the contemporary philosopher inclined toward physicalism, that your thinking is closely associated with some brain activity. Nonetheless we will not be able to locate that abstract object within your brain. Indeed, according to Augustine, $7 + 3 = 10$ is immutable and eternal, transcending the physical world entirely. If we are able to grasp it, it cannot be the case that we lay hold of it with, or store it in, a part of the body. $7 + 3 = 10$ is immaterial and the locus of our understanding of it must be immaterial as well.

Augustine provides a further proof based on introspection. He proposes it in the course of chiding those who see the soul as some kind of physical substance – maybe fire, or air, or some other element. The problem, says Augustine, is not that such philosophers are unfamiliar with what the soul is. We all have immediate, indubitable certitude that we exist, and live, and think. We all experience the thinking part of ourselves as soon as we attend to the operations of our own minds. The problem with the physicalists is that they insist upon adding something extraneous

to the soul. While they believe that the soul is air, or fire, or some other element, these philosophers cannot have certainty about which of these substances constitutes the soul. But since one can be in doubt about whatever physical description should apply to the soul, while experiencing the soul itself immediately and beyond any doubt, it must be the case that the soul is not any of those hypothesized substances. Rather it is the thinking aspect we recognize with certainty when we introspect.[12]

Aquinas proposes arguments for the incorporeal nature of the human soul, but we will not spell them out since they are largely dependent on his rather complex and difficult Aristotelian epistemology. The basic thought is that our natural knowledge comes through observation and understanding of the physical world around us. This means, says Aquinas, that our intellects are open to grasping any and every sort of body. But this entails that the intellect itself cannot be any particular body, nor an aspect of any body. Moreover, the intellect is able to grasp universal concepts, like the horseness of the horse. If the intellect were something material the concepts it holds would be only of individuals, since matter is the principle of individuation. Thus its activity is not the activity of any bodily parts. The rational soul, then, is incorporeal and subsistent.[13] Though it is a "part" of a complete human being, it is a thing which can exist on its own.

Augustine and Aquinas agree that there is no reason to hold that the death and corruption of the body entail the destruction of the soul. Is the immortality of the soul demonstrable (beyond the proof of heaven offered in the Introduction to this chapter)? In a couple of early works Augustine offers some very Platonic arguments for the immortality of the soul. (I suspect the contemporary reader is not likely to find them persuasive.) Truth is eternal. We know this since even if the universe around us ceased to exist, it would be *true* that it had ceased to exist. But it is the soul which grasps the truth, and therefore the soul must be eternal.[14] Further, the only possible cause of the soul's existence would have to be something superior to the soul, and that would be the purest and highest being. Since it enjoys the immediate causal presence of this purest and highest being, the soul cannot possibly lose its own being. It must be immortal.[15] (Would these arguments show that the soul must have existed forever in the past? That was Plato's view and some scholars have attributed it to the early Augustine. If he did indeed hold that position, he soon abandoned it.)

Aquinas gives several arguments for the immortality of the soul in Chapter 55 of Book 2 of his *Summa contra gentiles*. We will sketch a few here. They are based on his Aristotelian understanding of the soul as the form of the human being. He points out that what it means for anything

to be corrupted is for it to lose its form. For example, when a tree dies, its form, that is its "soul", what gave the tree being and life and made it the sort of thing it is, departs from that tree. The tree itself is no longer really a tree at all, and quickly decomposes.[16] If the human soul is indeed the form of the human being, but as incorporeal and subsistent, then it cannot possibly become corrupted, since it cannot lose its form. And so the soul is immortal.[17] Moreover, since it is form which bestows being on a thing, being is necessary to form as circularity is necessary to a circle. So a form which subsists, like the human soul, cannot possibly lose its being. It is form which "actualizes" a thing – gives it its nature and being – so there is no potentiality in the form itself – no capacity for becoming other than it is. But a corruptible thing must have within it the potentiality for corruption. So the soul is not corruptible. Again, what the human soul understands is necessary and incorruptible. Our knowledge begins with sense observation, but what we actually grasp of things is the immutable truth of their natures. That is what rational thought consists in. And since the soul must be able to conform to what it knows – what holds for the understanding, holds for what is understood – the soul must be immortal. And, as noted above, Aquinas holds that every intelligent being naturally desires its own continued existence. Since no natural desire can be in vain, the human soul must live forever.

Both Augustine and Aquinas take it that it is possible to mount philosophical arguments defending the human soul's incorporeal nature and its immortality. But even if this were not the case, it would be reasonable to believe these claims about the soul on faith, since there is no contradiction or incoherence here. It is the doctrine of the resurrection of the body that poses more of a stumbling block. Still, one could mount a sort of philosophical defense, even for this very problematic position, based on Aquinas's view of the human person. As noted in the argument for heaven, the human person naturally desires unending happiness. But no natural desire can be in vain. If the human person is a hylomorphic unity of soul and body, then after death, which is the separation of soul from body, the soul – even the soul of a saint – cannot reach its utmost fulfillment until it is reunited with its body. Therefore the body must be resurrected.[18] So the doctrine is entirely in keeping with the philosophical reasons for believing in the soul and its immortality. But both Augustine and Aquinas take the resurrection of the body to be a miraculous event to be accepted on faith. Christ's bodily resurrection shows us that this is how things work. But it is on faith that one believes in Christ's bodily resurrection.[19]

Augustine is confronted by Platonic philosophers who find the very thought of bodily resurrection absurd, and so he devotes some time in his

City of God to responding. These philosophers hold that death is a good thing, since it releases the good soul from the prison of the body. Augustine, who frequently expresses irritation with ivory tower, intellectual elitists, points out that our human experience is clearly one of body and soul closely intertwined. We experience death as the painful wrenching apart of what ought to be together.[20] Of course the body can cause problems for the person, but that is not due to the nature of the body per se, but rather due to sin.[21] Further, Augustine turns the Platonist's view against him by noting a puzzle that readers of Plato's work have been worried about since Plato's day. On Plato's account, in several of his dialogues (see, for example, the *Phaedo, the Republic,* and the *Timaeus*), the story is that the good immortal soul exists before it joins its current body, it survives the death of this body, is disembodied for a bit, and then finds itself thrust into a new body, and so on forever. But if the body is such a negative influence why in the world does the soul become embodied? Is it that the soul itself "longs" for the body? What is wrong with it that it should have such an unwholesome desire? Or is the soul thrust willy-nilly into a new body? Then what is wrong with the universe that such injustice should be perpetrated on lovely, innocent souls? Augustine points out that Plato's analysis of soul and body is just unsatisfactory, even on its own terms.

The debate continues because the Platonists hold that the very weight of the body and the elements of which it is composed make it too heavy to rise to heaven. Both they and Augustine seem to accept that heaven is in the sky, a view which the modern reader is likely to find naïve. We know a lot more about the sky than did Augustine, and we are used to traveling through parallel worlds, if only in fiction. The thought that you can get to heaven (or hell) in our physical universe by going far enough in the right direction seems misguided. We are more likely to assume that heaven and hell lie outside the bounds of our spatio-temporal world. Yes, it is a location, and yes, there is time (or something like time) there, but it is not accessible to even the very dedicated earthly traveler. But in any case, the Platonists need not worry about the weight of the body, says Augustine. Don't birds fly? Aren't human beings able to make craft that float out of materials that sink? Don't you Platonists hold that the lights dwelling in the heavens are embodied divinities? And don't you believe that the very earth itself is not resting "on" anything? God, in His omnipotence, will have no trouble at all raising the body to new life.[22]

What if the body has been pulverized? Even still, says Augustine, God can restore it.[23] Aquinas holds that it is the very fact of the body's decomposition that enables its reconstruction as a glorified body.[24] And there is no need to worry about the continuing survival of this exact bit of flesh or bone. As Aquinas notes, even in this earthly life, the material constituents of the body are not permanent but ebb and flow, yet the body is one, numerically same body over time.[25] But what about cannibalism when one person's body becomes a part of another person's body? Augustine and Aquinas both address the question, arguing roughly that it will be the person who had that body originally that will receive it at the resurrection. Aquinas does allow a qualification for multi-generational cannibals, but in any case, divine omnipotence is up to the task of sorting these things out.[26] That the body is resurrected must be believed, since Scripture is clear that Jesus was resurrected in the body, and in the very same body, in which he died. On the analysis that insists that human persons are body and soul combined, the thesis that you get your body back is central.

Life in the Afterlife

Upon death the soul is judged and bound for heaven or hell. Aquinas includes the thought that some souls, though due to achieve perfect beatitude, may still require purifying. These experience a period of purgatory before they are admitted to perfect union with God.[27] Those who enjoy beatitude – the saints – are able to gaze upon God directly. Augustine ends his discussion of heaven with the thought that the vision which the blessed will have of God is beyond human understanding.[28] Aquinas fills out the beatific vision a bit: the blessed experience delight in coming to know much of what God knows – what God has done, is doing, and will do. The limited creature can never fully comprehend God, so even the saints may not know all that God *could have done but didn't*, nevertheless, the human being's thirst for knowledge, especially knowledge of the natures of things, will be satisfied.[29] At the last judgment, a second process of judging occurs which involves the resurrection of the body. Now the saints will experience even greater joy, since now they are reunited with their bodies. Aquinas explains that after the resurrection the saints can know God intellectively through their souls, but also know God through His creation that is available to their senses.

Augustine and Aquinas both address questions concerning the embodied life after death, using scriptural statements as their guide. What age will one be? Probably around 30, the age at which Jesus died, that being the ideal age.[30] According to Augustine, it is reasonable to believe that even the unborn child who dies before birth has a human soul, and hence his body will be resurrected at the ideal age. How tall will one be? Just the right height. How much will one weigh? Just the right amount. The resurrected body will be glorified, and so will suffer no imperfection. Augustine holds that there is, for each person, an ideal height and weight relative to the prime of life for that person. The potentialities for developing to this proper condition exist from the beginning even in the "seed" of the new human being. And God will see to it that the glorified body is exactly what it ought to be.[31]

But if the resurrected body can have no defect, would that mean that women's bodies are not resurrected, since they are inferior to men's bodies? Apparently there were those in Augustine's day who raised this question. Augustine responds unequivocally. There is nothing defective about women and women's bodies. Of course their bodies will be resurrected the same as men's.[32] And, even though there will be no procreation of children in the afterlife, and no need to eat or drink, men's and women's bodies will have bodily integrity, that is, they will have all the parts that were natural for them to have in this life.[33] Augustine holds that, beyond insisting that it is the whole, same body that is resurrected at its proper age and height and weight, it is probably rash to try to describe what this glorified body will be like.[34] Aquinas, though, ventures a further description based on Scripture. The glorified body will be so agile that it will be able to move rapidly, though not instantaneously, in space. And it will – as Matthew 13:43 has it – shine like the sun. Aquinas cites a wonderful image from Wisdom 3:7, "The just shall shine and shall run to and fro like sparks among the reeds".[35] For further description of the brightly lit joy of heaven, see Dante's *Paradiso*.

Hell

Scripture and Church tradition teach that there is a hell and it is not empty. At death some souls are condemned to hell, and at the resurrection, the whole damned person, body and soul, is consigned to hell forever. The body suffers physical torments and the soul suffers spiritual torments, of which the worst is the everlasting separation from God. This is a difficult doctrine for the Christian thinker. If God is perfectly good and loving and also omnipotent, couldn't He see to it that everyone eventually becomes a saint? We pondered a related question in the chapter on grace. AAA agree that it is because of their freely chosen sins that some are damned. But we have seen in earlier chapters that Augustine and Aquinas are probably compatibilists when it comes to free will, while Anselm can be considered a libertarian. On the compatibilist understanding it is difficult to see why God would permit some souls to be eternally damned. The problem is not so much the question of how finite crimes could justify everlasting punishment. Both Augustine and Aquinas point out, quite rightly, that even when meting out earthly justice, we do not suppose that the time it took to commit the crime should determine the temporal length of the sentence. The crimes which merit eternal punishment are crimes against God. God is the infinite source of all, and so it is plausible that reason would require the greatest possible punishment. Moreover, committing damnable crimes damages and perverts the soul beyond recovery. The damned hate others, including God, and so inevitably remain the kind of people who are fit only for hell.[36]

I would argue that the problem of hell, for Augustine and Aquinas, stems from their understanding of created free will. (Their analysis of free will was discussed in the chapter on original sin.) Augustine and Aquinas hold that God is the cause of absolutely everything, including every creature's choice to sin. Nonetheless, they say, created agents are free because they are choosing in accord with their own desires – albeit the desires are God-given. The praiseworthiness and blameworthiness of created agents is thus compatible with God having caused them to choose what they choose. In causing a created agent to sin, God has not chosen wrongly, since that creaturely sin is part of the overall divine plan. God could have insured that all created agents would freely make good choices and go to heaven. This theory, that everyone winds up in heaven, is today called "Universalism". But AAA, based on Scripture and Church tradition, hold that God prefers that some should go to hell. Why? Augustine and Aquinas do offer reasons, but I suspect the charitably inclined reader will find them unappealing.

The dislike of hell is not a modern phenomenon. Augustine notes that many of his contemporaries, moved by compassion, prefer to say that the punishments undergone by the sinful have an end. Eventually all will arrive in heaven. He points out that, if his contemporaries want to be truly compassionate, they ought to want to see even Satan and his minions in heaven. And this is contrary to Scripture and a consequence that no one would find palatable, he assumes.[37] He expresses at least two purposes served by the souls in hell. In *On Free Will* the question arises of why God made those whom He knew would sin and never repent. In that dialogue his answer is that it is better for God to make all "levels" of souls – those who will never sin, those who will sin and repent, and those who will sin and not repent.[38] He seems to be trying to make hell an entailment of the principle of plenitude. This is a standard Medieval principle and figures importantly in *On Free Will*. It holds that the best universe is the one that contains the most different kinds of things possible. If this is the move Augustine is making, it is an abuse of the principle of plenitude. A sick or damaged member of a kind is not a different kind of being and – as the principle is usually understood – would add nothing to the order and beauty of the whole. For example, the Principle of Plenitude does not entail that it is better for there to be a limitless number of dogs, each suffering a different type or degree of illness. Augustine concludes his discussion in *On Free Will* with the thought that, in any case, it is better to exist than not, thus the never-to-repent should not complain at having been created.

Augustine offers another argument for the usefulness of the damned, and that is that their fate is necessary to exhibit divine justice.[39] Aquinas, too, defends hell as required by divine justice.[40] He makes a similar point in arguing that eternal punishment is required to maintain the order in the universe.[41] He goes even further, saying that the damned serve a purpose for the blessed in heaven who will appreciate witnessing divine justice in action and who will savor their own happiness more by comparison with the misery of the damned.[42] The modern reader is likely to find this last point especially unappetizing. It is one thing to appreciate divine justice but another to actively enjoy the suffering of the damned. And it is difficult to embrace Augustine's and Aquinas's point about divine justice, when both hold that it was God who caused the acts of sin by which the damned are damned. True, the damned chose as they chose through their own wills and based on their own desires. But God is the ultimate source of those desires and choices. Is it really just to cause someone to sin and then to punish them for it? Their understanding of Scripture and Church teaching do not allow Augustine and Aquinas the luxury enjoyed by some contemporary philosophers of religion of simply denying the existence of hell. And both adopt a compatibilist understanding of free will which supports their view of divine omnipotence, where God is the absolute source of all that exists and all that happens. If those pieces of the theoretical puzzle are held to be nonnegotiable, then Augustine's and Aquinas's attempts to explain the purpose or value of hell may be the best available. The reader may, however, see this as a good reason to reexamine the nature of free will and divine omnipotence.

Anselm never wrote a treatise on damnation, but arguably it is Anselm's analysis of created freedom that allows for the most adequate solution to the puzzle of God's allowing some to go to hell. For Anselm (see the chapter on original sin) it is the created agent, and not God, who causes the choice to sin. God allows created agents to make such choices because the only way to prevent them is to shut down the free will altogether. If the agent faces the genuinely open options necessary for real freedom and moral responsibility, then it must be possible that the agent opt badly. And some agents choose so badly, so consistently, that in effect, they choose to make their own way to hell. (Anselm makes this point most clearly in his *On the Fall of the Devil*.) Could God prevent the hellbound journey from reaching its conclusion? Anselm likely would hold that the most obvious way for God to prevent the sinner from achieving damnation is by annihilating the sinner. But God will not do this because, as Augustine had said, it is better to exist, even as a damned soul, than not to exist at all. The most fundamental value in Medieval thought is existence itself. All creatures reflect the being of God, and all things are good simply by being. God does not destroy a good thing.[43] But perhaps God could simply replace the libertarian free will of those who have abused it to the point of damnation with some form of compatibilist freedom by which God could draw them to heaven? On Anselm's account, this would deeply damage the created agent for whom libertarian freedom is part of what makes him a true image of God. It is better for the damned to exist as the extremely valuable kind of creatures they are than to cease to exist or to be so maimed that they are no longer free agents.[44] On Anselm's view hell is justified by the importance of created freedom.

Do all non-Christians go to hell? The next chapter, the last in this book, addresses how AAA understand the condition of those who do not share the Christian faith.

Notes

1 Anselm, *Monologion* 68–70; Aquinas, *Summa contra gentiles* (SCG) Book 2.55.13 and 79.6 and Book 3.48.11.

2 In Book 19 of the *City of God* Augustine makes it brutally clear why happiness cannot be had in this earthly life, except perhaps through hope for heaven. He offers a catalog of philosophers' attempts to find satisfaction in various earthly goods and shows why each and every one of them fails. Aquinas, SCG Book 3.48.

3 That a person has a rational soul doesn't entail that the person is reasoning. Infants, for example, have rational souls in that they possess the potential to become reasoning beings.

4 A prime example is ancient Atomism which originates before Socrates and has adherents for centuries: What there is, and all there is, is atoms drifting randomly in the void. The Atomists insisted that there is no need to invoke a designing God to explain why the universe is as it is. The view displayed a tough materialism and uncompromising simplicity that some temperaments find appealing. The Medieval philosophers by and large tended to reject Atomism. (Alghazali (1058–1111 CE) and some like-minded Islamic philosophers did accept a theistic version of the theory.) When atoms made a broad comeback in the modern period the theory was not taken to make God unnecessary.

5 The question of what instance of human life counts as an individual person is intimately related to the ethical question of what instances of human life deserve moral respect.

6 See, for example, Plato's *Republic, Phaedo,* and *Timaeus.*

7 *City of God* Book 13.

8 *On the Soul* Book 3.5.

9 *On the Trinity* Book 10.7.10, *Letter* 166.4. Aquinas, too, makes this argument. *Summa theologiae* (ST) 1 Q. 76 art. 8.

10 *On the literal meaning of Genesis* Book 7.20.26.

11 *On the literal meaning of Genesis* Book 7.21.28.

12 *On the Trinity* Book 10.7.10. This argument is striking in that it sounds similar to one which Descartes will offer more than a thousand years later. Aquinas disagrees with the argument. Since he holds that our natural knowledge begins with our senses, he does not think that introspection can uncover the nature of the soul to us. He says that Augustine must have meant that we are able to see *that* the soul exists, but not what it is (SCG Book 3.46.8). Augustine, though, is clear that he means to be describing the non-physical nature of the soul.

13 ST 1 Q. 75 arts. 2 and 5.

14 *Soliloquies* 2.23–24.

15 *On the Immortality of the Soul* 12.19.

16 Aristotle has it that the form of the tree never ceases to exist, since there have always been and will always be trees bearing the form. Aquinas agrees with Aristotle that the forms of things are in the things. He does not subscribe to the infinity of the earthly past or future, but he can hold that forms do not come into or pass out of being in any absolute way, since he can appeal to the eternal source of the form as an idea in the mind of God.

17 SCG Book 2.55.2.

18 SCG Book 4.79.10–11, ST *Supplement to the Third Part* (hereafter abbreviated, ST 3 *Supp.*) Q. 93 art. 1. If corruptionism is the correct theory of the interim situation of the soul, then the person who died will not even exist until soul and body are reunited.

19 Augustine, *On the Trinity* Book 13.12, *The City of God* 22.5; Aquinas, ST 3 *Supp.* Q. 75 art. 3.

20 *City of God* 13.6.

21 *City of God* 13.17.

22 *City of God* Book 22.

23 *City of God* Book 22.21.

24 ST 3 *Supp.* Q. 78 art. 2.

25 SCG Book 4.81.12, ST 3 *Supp.* Q. 80 art. 5.

26 Augustine, *City of God* Book 22.20; Aquinas, SCG Book 4.81.13, ST 3 *Supp.* Q. 80 art. 5. Since your body can survive replacement of all the actual bits that make it up, perhaps we do not need to worry too much about who has ingested which bits.

27 SCG Book 4.91.6. ST 3 *Supp.* Q. 71 art. 6.

28 *City of God* Book 22.29. Anselm emphasizes that the joy of being in the immediate presence of God is multiplied by the joy of sharing that beatific vision with all of the other saints whom one loves as one loves oneself (*Proslogion* 25).

29 SCG Book 3.59, ST 1 Q. 89.

30 Augustine, *City of God* Book 22.15; Aquinas, ST 3 *Supp.* Q. 81 art. 1.

31 *City of God* Book 22.14.

32 *City of God* Book 22.17; Aquinas, ST 3 *Supp.* Q. 81 art. 3.

33 Augustine, *City of God* Book 22.21; Aquinas, ST 3 *Supp.* Q. 80 arts. 1 and 4.

34 *City of God* Book 22.21.

35 ST 3 *Supp.* Q. 85 art. 1.

36 Augustine, *City of God* Book 21.11–12; Aquinas, SCG Book 3.144.4, ST 3 *Supp.* Q. 99 art. 1. Aquinas holds that the will of the deceased is "locked in" at death. Before death the will is joined to a corporeal body. If the will is pursuing the wrong ends this may be due to passions, habits, and cognitive processes associated with the body. Such bodily sources of misplaced desire are open to course correction. The same is not true after the separation of the soul from the body (SCG Book 4.95).

37 *City of God* Book 21.17.

38 *On Free Will* Book 3.5

39 *City of God* Book 21.12.
40 ST 3 *Supp.* Q. 94 art. 2 ad. 1 and art. 3 and Q. 99 art. 1.
41 SCG Book 3.140.5 and 144.9.
42 ST 3 *Supp.* Q. 94 art. 1 and Q. 99 art. 4.
43 In a surprising and, I would argue, uncharacteristic, passage Aquinas argues to the contrary that it would be better for the damned themselves for God to annihilate them. God does not do so because they serve the purposes we have mentioned above (ST 3 *Supp.* Q. 98 art. 3).
44 Augustine makes the point that it is better for the damned to lament their situation since that shows that at least traces of their good natures remain (*City of God* Book 19.13).

7

CHRISTIAN EXCLUSIVITY

Introduction

The last chapter ended with the question of whether, in the view of AAA, the non-Christian will go to hell. The short answer is "Yes". As set out in Chapter Two, AAA take it that all of humanity is infected with original sin. We neither deserve, nor are capable of, eternal beatitude. Happily, there is a cure. Chapter Three discussed how Christ's incarnation, passion, and death paid the debt for our sins. All we need to do is embrace Christ as our savior. Those who do not do so cannot enter heaven. Today many find this exclusivity offensive. The Christian claim to have the exclusive truth, they say, denotes intolerance and contempt for the other. But this is not a fair reading of AAA. Certainly, in accepting both the statements of the Church Councils and the laws of logic, AAA take the claims of Christian doctrine to be the case. The doctrines are true in a straightforward way that cannot admit that the contraries of these claims are also true. However, it does not follow that AAA hold that all of the views of non-Christians vis-à-vis the divine are mistaken.

Augustine, in terms of his metaphysics and epistemology, owes much to the Platonic and Neoplatonic tradition. And, as we will see, he defends Judaism, arguing against those who propose that the God of the Jews is not the Christian God. Anselm, in attempting to defend the Incarnation, assumes that those he is addressing, Jews and Muslims, share many of the fundamental beliefs of the Christian; the world was made by a good, omnipotent God who will see to it that the goal of humanity – eternal happiness – cannot fail. Aquinas has enormous respect for many non-Christian thinkers. His *Summa contra gentiles* is aimed at explaining the Catholic faith, and part of his methodology in setting out his understanding of God and creation, as he explains at the beginning of the work, is to appeal to natural reason which is shared by all of humanity.[1] In Aquinas's writing Aristotle is a major source, labeled "The Philosopher".

DOI: 10.4324/9781003202080-8

Though Aquinas expresses severe criticisms of Mohammed and Islam, he knows and uses the work of many Islamic thinkers, sometimes agreeing and sometimes disagreeing with them.[2] He borrows basic, important ideas from Ibn Sina (Avicenna) (980–1037 CE), notably the treatment of the fundamental metaphysical principles of essence and existence. He refers to Ibn Rushd (Averroes) (1126–1198 CE) respectfully as "The Commentator", in reference to Ibn Rushd's commentaries on Aristotle. Yet argues with him, for example, on the thesis that all of humanity shares one thinking mind. Aquinas also engages the great Jewish philosopher, Moses ben Maimon (Maimonides) (1138–1204 CE) frequently. Sometimes he argues against him, as when discussing the problem of how to talk about God, but sometimes he borrows Maimonides's solutions to long-standing problems, as when he addresses the issue of the eternity of the world. Thus Aquinas especially can be credited with a deep respect for non-Christian thinkers that played a central role in his philosophical and theological methodology.[3] But the fact remains, on the fundamental question of salvation AAA agree that it can only come through Christ.

AAA are deeply concerned to persuade those whom they take to be on the wrong track. The earlier chapters of this book discussed some of their efforts to explain and defend difficult doctrines against those who rejected them. Rather than canvassing their arguments against beliefs they take to be mistaken, the present chapter will set out their views on the problem of unbelief itself, and on how to treat non-Christians. We will concentrate on Augustine since he sets the tone for Anselm and Aquinas.[4] Augustine himself, as he records in his *Confessions,* embraced various philosophical positions and at least one major heresy, before he finally committed himself to Christianity. So he knew religious diversity from the inside. In his work he addresses pagans and adherents of a multitude of different philosophical schools. He also devotes a great deal of time to responding to Christian heresies. We will conclude the chapter with Augustine's very interesting writings on the Jews and Judaism, which influenced thinkers, including Aquinas, throughout the Middle Ages.

We will not examine the question of AAA's attitude toward the treatment of Muslims. They say much less about Muslims than about heretics and Jews. Augustine has nothing at all to say about Muslims, since Muhammed, the founder of Islam, was born after Augustine had died. Muhammed was born in the mid-sixth century, and by the eighth century Islam had spread by military conquest all the way from Spain in the west to India in the east, including parts of southern Italy, North Africa, and the Middle East. Christians in Europe would have thought of Muslims as military adversaries. Augustine does famously defend the thought that waging war can be just under certain circumstances.[5] His arguments might defend the crusades that started in the eleventh century, in that the justification, in the eyes of Christian Europeans, was to prevent further incursions by Islamic armies, to take back the Holy Land, and to liberate Christians persecuted under Muslim rule. But we probably cannot construct an educated opinion on what Augustine might have said about the treatment of Muslims. Anselm's attempt to respond to critics of Christianity in his *Cur deus homo* may be in part directed at Muslims as well as Jews, but beyond that his views are not expressed in his philosophical or theological work. (There is some reason to believe he was not enthusiastic about the First Crusade called in 1095 by Urban II, but his concern is a very specific one related to taking monks on crusade.[6]) Aquinas, as mentioned above, was critical of Islam but impressed by the philosophical and theological acumen of his Islamic predecessors. By Aquinas's day crusading was standard practice for European armies. Aquinas reviews Augustine's arguments for when a war is just and presumably held that the crusades were fought in defense of unjustly seized or threatened Christian lands and unjustly oppressed Christian populations.[7] But regarding the treatment of individual Muslims, neither Anselm nor Aquinas offers a clear statement. So we will concentrate on what Augustine and Aquinas have to say about heretics and Jews.

Grace and Baptism

Before going further, it is well to discuss grace and baptism as related to exclusivity. As discussed in Chapter Four, AAA agree that grace is necessary for salvation. What this means is that anyone might be saved. Regarding our fellow human beings, we simply do not know what their destiny is. The most vicious dictator, the most unyielding atheist, may be bound for glory. AAA do all hold – based on scriptural evidence – that baptism is required for salvation. But, as it turns out, anyone can baptize. There had been debate in Augustine's day. The Donatists (about whom more below) had argued that only *virtuous* churchmen could baptize. Augustine, ever the opponent of elitism, argued that, no, what is vital is that the correct form is followed. The moral status of the particular churchman in question is irrelevant to the success of the sacrament. In fact, the one baptizing need not be a churchman, or even a man.[8] But doesn't the one baptizing at least have to be a Christian? Aquinas notes that Augustine was not sure whether the one baptizing has to be a Christian. Aquinas goes on to point out that by his own day the issue had been decided; even a non-Christian can baptize.[9] But, asks Aquinas, what about the person who has lived all his life in the jungle, away from anyone who could teach him about Christ and baptize? If, through his good works, he shows himself worthy, then God will send someone to him. And, of course, those good works will be the result of divine grace.[10] Today the Catholic Church, upholding the necessity of baptism, has continued the movement toward a very broad understanding of the availability of baptism. One seeking to become a Christian, who dies before baptism, can be saved through their explicit desire to receive the sacrament. One who has no access to Christian teaching, but who truly attempts to follow the will of God, can be saved in that, had he known of the necessity of baptism, he would have desired it.[11]

AAA uphold the thought that the apparent non-Christian may nonetheless be saved through Christ by grace. On the other hand, not everyone who claims to be a Christian will escape hell. In Augustine's *City of God* he divides humanity into those who are heaven-bound, the City of God, and those who are not, the City of the World. But he is clear that not all Christians, and not all churchmen, belong to the City of God.[12] In Augustine's day there were those who argued that simply holding the correct beliefs about God and Christ would secure their salvation. No, says Augustine, faith without works is dead. Some added the thought that, no matter what else you do, so long as you participated in the sacraments (such as baptism, the eucharist, etc.) that assured your eternal beatitude. No, says Augustine. Some suggested that the inveterate criminal could win heaven by giving enough to charity. But, No, says Augustine. One cannot secure eternal happiness through outward practice.[13]

We simply do not know who will go to heaven and who will not. The chapter on grace pointed out that, according to Augustine, even if one had felt the effects of grace, especially in the desire to pursue justice and in finding it easy to do, one could not have *certainty* that one will be saved. And this is psychologically a good thing, he argues, since otherwise one might be tempted to pride and to becoming lazy. Moreover, since we do not know who, in the final analysis, is a citizen of the City of God, we must try to treat everyone as if they might be. How should we treat the non-Christian?

Pagans, Philosophers, and Heretics

We will use the term "pagan" for those who worshipped other gods than the Christian God. So, for example, those who worshipped the gods of Greece or Rome were pagans. Being a pagan and being a philosopher might or might not overlap. A philosopher (for our purposes) is one who attempts, through reason, to build a theory about the nature of the universe and humanity's place in it. There were, in Augustine's day, an abundance of non-Christian (even anti-Christian) philosophers of various sorts. Some would have given at least lip service to traditional gods and some were explicitly atheists. Augustine deals with the pagans and the philosophers through argument. The *City of God* was written largely as a response to the claims of Roman pagans that the fall of Rome was caused by so many citizens abandoning the gods of Rome in favor of the Christian God. And throughout his enormous body of work Augustine mounts arguments against a host of non-Christian philosophers. Against the Skeptics, for example, he presents his famous claim that human beings are capable of knowing some things with certainty by pointing out that, "Even if I am deceived, I exist".[14] Against the Stoics, who held that one could achieve happiness in this life, he notes that the goods of this life inevitably fail to offer the deep, total happiness we long for.[15] And in the previous chapter we discussed Augustine's responses to those Platonists who found the Christian doctrines of the Incarnation and bodily resurrection absurd.[16] The pagans and the philosophers can be met with argument. Heretics, however, are a different matter.

Both Augustine and Aquinas hold that it is legitimate for the Church to request that the state use its power against heresy.[17] Sometimes it may even be appropriate for the secular power to put the heretic to death. The contemporary citizen of a liberal western democracy is likely to find this stance fundamentally morally wrong. Today the Catholic Church defends religious liberty as a basic, natural right.[18] But before we heap too much blame on Augustine and Aquinas we need to appreciate what they actually said, and, before that, a few general remarks are in order. It is often believed that the Middle Ages in Western Europe was an unusually brutal period in human history, and its brutality stemmed from the ascendency of the Catholic Church. But note, first, that plenty of people on planet Earth at the present moment are persecuted and even killed for their religious beliefs. Moreover, the number of heretics persecuted and killed during the medieval period pales in comparison to the millions of innocent citizens killed by their own governments in the twentieth century in pursuit of the utopian visions of the likes of Hitler and Stalin and Mao. That does not justify the deaths of the heretics, but it does suggest that there is nothing uniquely medieval about governments killing people unjustifiably. And sometimes the historically innocent believe that the medieval Church invented religious persecution. On the contrary, persecuting and killing people of other religions (or nonconforming members of one's own religion) has been standard human behavior from time immemorial. For example, as Christianity began to spread within the Roman Empire, large numbers of Christians were brutally persecuted and killed. The last great persecution of Christians was ordered by the Emperor Diocletian at the beginning of the fourth century, within living memory in

Augustine's day. (Shortly thereafter the Edict of Milan in 313 made it legal to be a Christian.) Medieval people (with the possible exception of the Vikings whose job it was to raid and murder and rape and pillage) were not more bloodthirsty than the rest of humanity before and after the Middle Ages. (For one explanation of ubiquitous human wickedness see the chapter on original sin.) And remember, it was Western Christendom in the medieval period that gave us almshouses (i.e. homes for the poor supported by charity), hospitals, and universities. Even though we assume they were mistaken, what Augustine and Aquinas say about the treatment of heretics is moderate and thoughtful in the context of their times and in the context of world history in general.

First, what is a heretic? Augustine, in a late work, *On Heresies*, listing numerous heretical views, points out that it would be impossible to offer a detailed definition of heresy that would both include every position that is properly labeled heresy and exclude other anomalous positions that should not be considered heretical. He does explain several general attributes that we can apply to the heretic. First, the heretic must claim to be a Christian. On Augustine's understanding he cannot be a *Catholic* Christian. "Catholic" means universal, and someone who holds fast to the teaching of the universal Church is not a heretic. But someone who self-identifies as any variety of *non*-Christian cannot possibly be a heretic, either. Second, he must adhere to a doctrine that contradicts that of the Church on an issue that is important and relevant to the faith. Third, it must be the case that a proper authority has explained to the heretic that his views do not cohere with the doctrines of the Church. Farmer Jones, out in the field, may believe a claim that contradicts Church teaching, but if no one has pointed this out to him, he is not a heretic. And finally, having been shown that his position opposes that of the Church, he must persist in holding it. Someone who renounces his private claim once he is shown that it contradicts Church teaching ceases to be a heretic. The heretic can easily become a schismatic, that is one who leaves the main body of the Church and, as often as not, pulls his followers along with him. Augustine considered the unity of the believers in Christ to be very important, thus he took heresy and schism to be fundamentally harmful to Christianity in general and to Christians as individuals.

Augustine confronted three major heresies during his lifetime; Manicheanism, named after Mani, a religious leader, Pelagianism named after Pelagius, and Donatism, named after Donatus. We will look at Augustine's battles against heretics in that order. Augustine had been a Manichean for almost ten years before he converted to Christianity. Manicheanism, while claiming to be the true Christianity, held a cosmic dualism. There are two equal and opposite divinities eternally at war in the universe.

There is a good force or god and a bad force or god. The good is associated with light and spirit (a sort of bright, aethereal matter), while the bad is associated with dark, corporeal matter. Human beings are the battleground between these two forces, since we are soul – a spark of the divine – trapped in the evil, earthly body. Procreation is bad since it traps more of the divine in the evil matter. Death is a good, since it releases the good soul from the prison of the body. It is the bad divinity who is represented as god in the Old Testament. The Jews are worshippers of this evil god, as their carnal behavior, such as offering animal sacrifice, shows. Christ did not actually take on a human body. The good god would not do such a gross thing! Jesus was not actually descended from David, and he and his followers did not follow the old Jewish law. Jesus was not resurrected bodily, since he didn't really have a body. Granted there are many texts in the Gospels and Apostolic letters which seem to say otherwise, but, said the Manicheans, they must have been added after the fact by false Christians who did not understand how purely spiritual Christianity ought to be.[19]

The Manichean claims oppose central Christian teachings. The Old Testament is to be entirely rejected and the New Testament, as we find it, is full of errors. The views that the body is evil, and that Jesus could not have been embodied, have all sorts of ramifications. The human person is really the spirit, imprisoned in the nasty flesh. The practice of medicine and general concern for the body are misguided. Having children is evil because it traps more of the divine spirit in the gross matter. Death is good as the final separation of the soul from the body.

Augustine eventually rejected Manicheanism.[20] His main philosophical reason was that he realized that if the good god of the Manicheans could never defeat the evil god, then he wasn't much of a god at all. Moreover, Augustine, through reading "the books of the Platonists", found a more satisfactory answer to the problem of evil than that which the Manicheans offered. For the Manicheans the physical universe was just bad and made by the bad god. The Platonists inspired Augustine's famous "privative" theory of evil. Evil is not base matter, or any kind of stuff or substance. It is a lack, a corruption, a destruction, a falling away from the good. The good God is omnipotent and the source of all, and evil is just an absence of good, having no positive being at all. Augustine subsequently devoted much of his work to answering the Manicheans.[21] And the Catholic Church from Augustine's day to ours has argued against those who would denigrate the human body.

Augustine's debate with the Pelagians was discussed in the chapter on divine grace. The Pelagians held that grace was not necessary for salvation. Original sin had not done so much damage that no one could merit heaven through their own free will. Maybe most people do need grace, but "we" (certain members of the wealthy, elite class of Romans), if we try very hard, can be good enough on our own to deserve eternal beatitude. Augustine argued that this position undermines divine omnipotence by suggesting that God *owes it* to the self-perfected to save them because, by their own choices, they deserve it. Moreover, it makes Christ's incarnation, crucifixion, and resurrection pointless. Why would God engage in such a bizarre and circuitous project for our salvation if humanity didn't really need it? Augustine's work succeeded in eclipsing Pelagianism within the Catholic Church, though problems of grace and free will have persisted to the present day.

In Augustine's writings against the Pelagians and the Manicheans we do not find the suggestion that the power of the state should be invoked against them.[22] It is against Donatism, a North African schism, that Augustine holds that it may be legitimate to use force to stop heresy and reconvert the heretics. Above I mentioned the Diocletian persecution of the early fourth century, the last great persecution of Christians in the Roman Empire. During that persecution some Christian churchmen, to save their lives, had handed over sacred books to the Romans. Others had instead chosen death in order to protect the books. Once the persecutions were well over and Christianity was legalized, the Donatists argued that those churchmen who had sacrificed the sacred books were not worthy to administer the sacraments. They were labeled *traditores* from the Latin, *to hand over*, from which we get our English word "traitor". The Donatists held that someone baptized by one of these *traditores* would have to be re-baptized, since baptism by a wicked traitor could not be efficacious. As the Donatist sect grew it became a true schism, dividing the Church in North Africa. Some among the Donatists resorted to violence, attacking Catholic Churches. Doctrinally the Donatists were closer to Catholic Christians than were the Pelagians, and much closer than were the Manicheans. But in practical terms, had the universal Church embraced their understanding of the clergy and the sacraments, it would have been devastating for Christendom. It is impossible to know the moral status of anyone. If the sacraments, including and especially baptism, are effective only when administered by the pious, one could never be sure that one had truly received a sacrament.

Furthermore, the Donatists fall prey to a vice that can damn them and their followers. They hold that they are the true Church of the martyrs. Only they are pure enough to perform the sacraments. Outside of their churches Christendom has failed, since all those others are not good enough to carry on the faith. The thought that you, and your select band of followers, are the only true Christians, because of your own pious behavior, is pride. One thing all three of these heresies that Augustine attacked have in common is that they are religions for the elite, those who see themselves as superior to the mass of mankind. The Manicheans held that their commitment to the spiritual set them apart from the rest of carnal humanity. The Pelagians said some (of them) could be good enough to rise to heaven on their own without the grace that the "masses" might require. The Donatists considered only themselves pure enough to constitute the Church. Augustine consistently opposes elitism. His doctrine of grace absolutely levels the playing field regarding eternal destinies. In terms of salvation he is the hero of the common man.

Augustine reports that earlier in his career he had disapproved of the state's use of force against heretics. It seemed that one could not force someone to believe something, and trying to do so would just encourage false claims to have renounced heresy. That might fill the Church with people who only pretended to hold the Catholic faith, and that could damage the Church. Later, Augustine says, he came to see that coercive measures taken by the state could work to tamp down heresy and restore unity to the Church. They had, in fact, worked against segments of the Donatists. And the Church, he says, is strong enough to survive a few pretenders.[23] Scholars debate the overall motivation for Augustine's change of attitude, but we can mention a few points. Regarding the justification for the existence of a government, Augustine's view is pessimistic (or *realistic*, depending on your political philosophy). According to Augustine the very existence of the state is a punishment for sin. He is thinking of government especially as those authorized to use force within the community. We would not have needed the soldiers with the swords if not for original sin. But under the circumstances, the state is necessary to keep order. That is its job.[24] Schism within the Church causes disorder intrinsically, and the tension between the Donatists and the Catholics had turned violent. That the state would step in and repress the schismatics was, in Augustine's view, a salutary move. And Augustine holds that those who cut themselves off from the Catholic faith are (in all likelihood) cutting themselves off from salvation. Augustine's analogy is seeing someone you know who, because of a mistaken belief, voluntarily jumps into a well to commit suicide. Augustine thinks you would have every right to pull him out, even against his will.[25] It is an act of charity toward the heretic and those he seeks to convert to require him – even to force him – to stop proclaiming his divisive view. We may disagree with Augustine's defense of coercion against heretics, but we should be able to understand it.

Aquinas, too, holds that the state may use its power to stamp out heresy. The heresy with which he was most concerned was Albigensianism, of which the fundamental tenets were similar to Manicheanism. There are two "gods" at war in the universe, the good and the evil. The evil god is associated with matter and is the one who made the nasty human body. The Old Testament's god is the god of evil, and Christ did not take on a human body. The Albigensian community was divided into the few "perfect ones" who lived very austere lives, and everyone else, the "believers". If, before death, one received the final sacrament at the hands of a perfect one, one was guaranteed release from the evil body and a purely spiritual salvation.

Albigensianism began to appear in Western Europe in the eleventh century and to spread and flourish in southern France and northern Italy. In the twelfth century a Spanish priest, Domingo de Guzman (St. Dominic), founded an order of preachers, the Dominicans, who were to travel around the areas falling under Albigensian influence and persuade the heretics to return to the Catholic Church. The attempts to persuade failed, and early in the thirteenth century there followed an ugly crusade against the Albigensians which degenerated into a murderous land grab by nobles from the north of France. The conquerors seized what had been Albigensian lands, the influence of the heresy was destroyed, and it died out by the end of the fourteenth century.

Aquinas, born in 1225, was impressed by the Dominicans. They lived very simply, not amassing any wealth, and exercised their intellectual skills in the name of charity. He became a Dominican, defending the faith through a life of teaching and writing. Though the Albigensians were no longer a major threat in Aquinas's day, he was concerned to counter the problem of heresy. He agrees with Augustine that it is legitimate for the state to exercise its power against heresy, even to the point of killing the heretic. And his motivations are similar to those we attributed to Augustine; schism within the Church is destructive, not just to peace within the Church, but to social order in general. Moreover, in charity, the heretic must be prevented from harming himself and others. Aquinas adds an analogy between the heretic and the forger. Both are passing off falsehood as if it were true, but the latter is falsifying only the currency while the former is falsifying the faith. Our (thirteenth century) law allows for the execution of forgers, so much the more should it allow for the execution of heretics. They deserve the severest punishment even more than does the forger.[26]

Augustine had recorded a tension in his own thinking between the importance of respect for the individual's free decisions and the value of averting schism within the Church. In Aquinas's work this tension – though not underscored by Aquinas himself – is more pronounced. Aquinas, in various places, emphasizes the importance of conscience. "Conscience" is your ability to tell right from wrong when deciding what you ought to do or assessing the moral status of what you have done.

Aquinas holds that you are "bound" by your conscience. If you judge some action to be the right thing to do, then you should do it. And this is true even if you are making a mistake. If you believe, through no fault of your own, that something is right to do, even though objectively it is not, you are morally bound to do it. If you choose contrary to this mistaken deliverance of your conscience, you might act in the way that is objectively right, but nonetheless you have sinned, since you did what you believed to be wrong.[27] Aquinas does not connect his points about conscience to the problem of heresy, but the application is obvious. One who sincerely, through no fault of their own, believes that the non-Catholic doctrine is the truth is morally bound to defend it. Aquinas's analogy between the forger and the heretic seems to fail in the case of the *honest* heretic. He is bound in conscience to maintain his non-Catholic views. And then it is hard to see that he *deserves* execution, even if the heresy must be stamped out in the interests of social order. Aquinas might respond that one is a heretic only if one persists in clinging to his own views after it has been explained to him that he is contradicting the teachings of the Church. And, Aquinas could continue, valuing your own cognitive abilities more than Church teaching and placing your own beliefs above those of the Church could only be due to pride.[28] So perhaps he would see the "honest" heretic as a straw man not a live possibility. Still, his clear insistence that one must follow one's conscience seems in tension with his defense of the state's use of force against heretics. While we today are likely to disagree with Augustine and Aquinas regarding the treatment of heretics, their views do not stem from ignorance or malice. In the places and times and contexts in which they are working their voices are, by comparison with those around them, moderate and thoughtful.

The Jews

The Jews are not heretics. What then is their status and how should they be treated? Augustine, in his controversy with the Manicheans, developed an understanding of the importance of the Jewish community which was both positive and influential. Of course, in not recognizing Jesus as the Savior they are making a terrible mistake, a mistake that is damning if not abandoned before death. And they have less excuse than other non-Christians since they have had access to knowledge of Christ's coming, before the fact, through the prophets. Augustine certainly does not think everything is fine with the Jews. Nonetheless, in the context of history, he is their champion.

In discussing Manicheanism above I noted that the Manicheans believed that the god represented in the Jewish Scripture (the Old

Testament) was the evil god. The Jews were worshippers of this evil god, essentially the Devil. The evil god made the nasty, corporeal side of the universe, and that is why the Jews engage in an offensive, carnal sort of worship, for example offering bloody animal sacrifice to their god. Christ, being good, did not assume a human body. He was pure spirit. And so He was most certainly not a Jew. All of those statements in the Gospels and the apostolic letters seeming to say that Christ was a member of the Jewish community were misinterpreted or just added later by people who wanted to subvert the pure (Manichean) faith.

Augustine points out, at length and emphatically, that all of this is just nonsense. His main target is Faustus, a Manichean bishop, whom Augustine had met when he was still a Manichean. He writes a long work, *Against Faustus*, in which he quotes Faustus extensively and then responds. The Manicheans claimed to take their understanding of Christ and his work from the Christian Scriptures, but then, points out Augustine, their methodology of picking and choosing which texts to accept and which to reject based simply on which they can bend to suit their dualistic philosophy is bankrupt. The text is clear. Jesus is born to a Jewish mother in a Jewish family. They follow the Jewish law. For example, Jesus was circumcised on the eighth day after his birth. (The Manicheans found circumcision to be an especially nasty expression of Jewish carnality!) Jesus's life and work takes place within the Jewish community and all of his original followers are Jewish.

But there is more. One cannot divorce Christ from the Jewish Scriptures that prophesy His coming. And what those Scriptures make clear is that God especially chose the Jews from among all the nations to be the community within which the Messiah would come. And, in spite of having rejected Jesus, the Jews are still under the special protection of God. How do we know? The Jews have been dispersed throughout the world, especially after the destruction of the temple in Jerusalem (70 CE). And yet, unlike other peoples who have been uprooted and forced to live among strangers, they have not abandoned their unique identity and practices. Why would God continue to protect them? For one thing, He promised to do so, and would not break His promise. But also, continues Augustine, there is a special purpose served by the communities of Jews throughout the world. Wherever they go they take their holy books with them. Their books attest to the divine plan for mankind's salvation. They do so through the law which prefigures Christ's work and through the prophets who predict His coming. The Jews do not interpret their Scriptures this way, but their holy books testify to the truth of Christianity. Those one hopes to convert might have thought that the ancient evidence for the divine plan of salvation was made up by the Christians.

But when they see that the books of the enemies of Christianity foretell the coming of Christ, would-be converts will be more likely to accept that evidence of the truth of Christianity. Eventually the Jews will convert to Christianity, and that will signal the end of the world. In the meantime they are still "chosen" by God and serve an important purpose as witnesses to the divine plan. In the *City of God* (18.46) Augustine repeated this thought, quoting Psalm 59 regarding the Jews, "Slay them not lest they forget your law; scatter them by your might". This is Augustine's "witness" doctrine, well-known to Medieval intellectuals. To give a striking example: In 1146 Bernard of Clairvaux invoked the doctrine, quoting Psalm 59, and his intervention apparently saved Jewish lives from crusaders who thought to kill European Jews before going on to liberate the Holy Land.[29]

Aquinas, too, embraces the witness doctrine. The Jews, dispersed through the world and bearing their books, give evidence of the truth of Christianity. He expands on it in his commentary on Paul's *Letter to the Romans*, especially Chapters 9–11. He reviews and dismisses the Manichean claim that Jesus was not born in a human body. On the contrary the savior was born from the Jews, and only to the Jews did God incarnate come in person. Aquinas repeatedly quotes John 4:22, "Salvation is from the Jews". The pre-Christian Jews are God's chosen people. Yes, the Jews have sinned. They are, as Paul says, the "old branches" ripped off the olive tree so that the "new branches", believers in Christ, can be grafted on. But Christians must not boast. They are still supported by the roots of the tree, that is Judaism out of which the new faith grows. And, in any case, if one judges oneself to be among the saved, remember that this is due to the grace of God, which is open to everyone. Rather than boasting against those who have fallen, one should fear for oneself lest pride cause one's own fall. One should pray for those who are not in communion with the Church and hope for their welfare. This is especially apt concerning the Jews since they are protected by God, and it is their conversion that will mark the end times. From the perspective of the twenty-first century, the Jewish person may judge that the witness doctrine is demeaning; the purpose of the Jews is to unwittingly serve the Christian Church. But, in context, Augustine and Aquinas were defending the Jewish community by responding to those who viewed the Jews as devil-worshippers, and, in practice, appeal to the witness doctrine saved Jewish lives in the Middle Ages.

The Christianity of AAA is exclusivist. We are all infected with sin and Christ is the only means of salvation. That is what Christians have traditionally believed. The contemporary reader is likely to hold that this exclusivity takes a wrong turn when we see Augustine and Aquinas defending use of coercion by the state against heretics or when they hold that the "purpose" of the Jewish community is to bear witness to the truth of Christianity. Today most people of good will in western democracies take it for granted that we should respect those belonging to faiths different from our own and act accordingly. But regarding respect, note that for AAA their main approach to non-Christians of any persuasion is to *argue with them*. AAA take the beliefs of their opponents seriously. As should be clear from the earlier chapters of this book, all of them devote enormous amounts of time and energy to discussing the debated issues. First they try to set out their opponents positions honestly and clearly. For example, in *Against Faustus* cited above, Augustine devotes pages and pages *and pages* to quoting Faustus verbatim. Or take Anselm's defense of the necessity of the Incarnation. It begins with a sympathetic statement of the opponents claim that the doctrine is absurd and demeaning to God, and Anselm clearly grasps the power of this claim. And the whole structure of Aquinas's *Summa theologiae* gives credit to those he disagrees with by starting every question with a list of possible objections to the view he will defend. AAA go on to criticize the positions they disagree with, but in doing so they assume that their opponents are their intellectual equals, capable of following the argument and perhaps changing their views. AAA devoted most of their lives to honest philosophical and theological debate; reasoned argument back and forth about issues of grave import. The very act of engaging in such debate expresses deep charity and fundamental respect for the opponent.

Conclusion

Christianity is a religion of difficult doctrines like the Trinity and the Incarnation. I have tried to suggest how three great Christian thinkers, Augustine, Anselm, and Aquinas (AAA), defend these doctrines against the charge of incoherence or (in the case of this last chapter) moral failure. Their work is vital to the health of Christianity since many people will not embrace a faith that they hold to be irrational or fundamentally meaningless or intolerant. AAA are operating at the highest level of philosophical expertise and producing explanations that are complex and demanding intellectually. But here at the end of outlining some of their challenging answers to the "hard questions" of Christianity it is well to remember that all of them shared the same basic faith commitment of the simplest believer: Out of love, the Son of God became a man who died to save us from our sins so that we might enjoy eternal happiness with Him in heaven. Jesus Christ is the immovable center around which all of AAA's brilliant philosophy and theology revolves. Difficult though the philosophical and theological underpinnings may be, can you imagine a more joyous picture of the universe and humanity's place in it?

Notes

1 *Summa contra gentiles* (SCG) Book 1.2.
2 He argues that, unlike Christianity, Islam spread by force of arms (SCG Book 1.6 art.4).
3 St. John Paul II notes this in his papal encyclical *Fides et Ratio* (Daughters of St. Paul, 1998) 57–58.
4 Anselm has very little to say about the treatment of non-Christians in his philosophical writing. It is probably safe to say that he was in rough agreement with Augustine.
5 *Against Faustus* Book 22.73–79.
6 R.W. Southern, *Saint Anselm: A Portrait in a Landscape* (Cambridge: Cambridge University Press, 1990) 252.
7 *Summa theologiae* (ST) 2–2 Q. 40 art. 1. In art. 2 obj. 2 Aquinas mentions "the Saracens" (Muslims), so clearly they are included in his discussion of the just war.
8 *Against the Letter of Parmenian* 2.
9 ST 3 Q.67 art.3.
10 *Commentary on Romans* Chapter 10, Lecture 3.
11 *Catechism of the Catholic Church* Sections 1257–1261.
12 *City of God* Book 18.49.
13 *City of God* Book 21.20–27.
14 *City of God* Book 11.26
15 *City of God* Book 19.4
16 *City of God* Book 22.11
17 Anselm wrote against the heretic Roscelin who denied the orthodox understanding of the Trinity, but, to my knowledge, he does not express himself on the treatment of heretics in general.
18 *Catechism of the Catholic Church* Sections 2107–2109.
19 For Augustine's description of Manicheanism see his *On Heresies* 46 and *Against Faustus*. The former offers a short overview, while the latter records a lengthy debate with Faustus, a well-known Manichean bishop.
20 *Confessions* Book 7.
21 See for example, his *On Free Will* as well as *Against Faustus*.
22 Towards the end of the fourth century paganism was outlawed in the Empire, and Augustine does not seem to have objected to the state's use of force to stamp it out.
23 *Letter 93, to Vincentius*, especially section 17. For his earlier disapproval of force against heretics see *On True Religion* 16.31.
24 *City of God* Book 19.17.
25 *Letter* 173.
26 ST 2–2 Q. 11 art. 3.
27 *On Truth* Q. 17.4.
28 ST 2–2 Q. 11 art. 1 ad 2.
29 Paula Fredriksen, *Augustine and the Jews* (New York, NY: Doubleday, 2008) xi.

BIBLIOGRAPHY

Primary Sources

Works by Augustine, Anselm, Boethius, and Aquinas are available in many English translations on paper and online. Good translations that are readily available include:

Anselm of Canterbury, *Anselm of Canterbury: The Complete Treatises*, edited and translated by Thomas Williams (Indianapolis, IN: Hackett Publishing Company, 2022).

Augustine of Hippo, *The Works of Saint Augustine: A Translation for the 21ˢᵗ Century*, (Hyde Park, NY: New City Press, 1990–)) (Series now has 44 volumes. To find the correct volume for a specific text check your library listing of contents, or see *Augustine through the Ages*, listed below under "Encyclopedias".)

Boethius, *The Consolation of Philosophy*, translated by Victor Watts (London: Penguin Classics, 1999).

Thomas Aquinas, (online) *isidore.co/aquinas*. (Texts originally compiled by Fr. Joseph Kenny, O.P., 1936-2013. Includes Latin opposite English.)

Encyclopedias and Handbooks

Augustine through the Ages: An Encyclopedia, general editor Allan D. Fitzgerald, O.S.A. (Grand Rapids, MI: William B. Eerdmans Publishing Company, 1999). (Pages xxxv–xlii list Augustine's works and English translations.)

Oxford Encyclopedia of the Middle Ages, edited by Andre Vauchez (Oxford: James Clarke & Co., (print) 2002, (online) 2005).

Oxford Handbook of Philosophical Theology, edited by Thomas P. Flint and Michael C. Rea (Oxford: Oxford University Press, 2009).

Stanford Encyclopedia of Philosophy, co-principal editors, Edward N. Zalta and Uri Nodelman, https://plato.stanford.edu.

The Catholic Encyclopedia (1913) https://www.newadvent.org>cathen.

Other Sources

Catechism of the Catholic Church: Revised in Accordance with the Official Latin Text Promulgated by Pope John Paul II, Second Edition (Washington, D.C.: United States Catholic Conference, 2019).

Fredriksen, Paula, *Augustine and the Jews* (New York, NY: Doubleday, 2008).

John Paul II, *Fides et Ratio* (Boston, MA: Daughters of St. Paul, 1998)

Rogers, Katherin, *Anselm on Freedom* (Oxford: Oxford University Press, 2008).

Rogers, Katherin, *Freedom and Self-Creation: Anselmian Libertarianism* (Oxford: Oxford University Press, 2015).

Southern, R.W., *Saint Anselm: A Portrait in a Landscape* (Cambridge: Cambridge University Press, 1990).

Tanner, Norman P., *Decrees of the Ecumenical Councils* Two-Volume Set (Washington, D.C.: Georgetown University Press, 1990).

Torrell, Jean-Pierre, *Saint Thomas Aquinas,* translated by Robert Royal (Washington, D.C.: Catholic University Press (Vol. 1) 1996 and (Vol. 2) 2003).

INDEX

corruptionism *see* personal identity
after death
Councils, Church: Ecumenical 15;
and the Holy Spirit 14–15, 16,
18; importance of 14–16; and
interpreting Scripture 14; *see also*
Chalcedon; Nicaea
creation, divine 3, 7–8, 19–20
crusades 116–117

damnation *see* hell
Dante's *Paradiso* 109
death 20, 46, 53, 99, 101, 103,
107, 121
Descartes 113n12
Devil 44, 63, 64, 67–68, 110, 126
Diocletian persecution 119–120, 122
Dionysius, Pseudo- 27n28
Divine Command Theory 4
Dominic, St. 124
Donatism 117, 120, 122–123

elitism 123
emotions, divine 7
empiricism, Aquinas's 10, 11, 36, 67,
70, 81, 102
equivocal language *see* language
applied to God
eternalism *see* time
eternality, divine 6–7, 91, 93, 94–95
evil 4, 8, 43–44, 88; moral 45, 88–89;
natural 44–45; privative theory of
44, 121; purpose of 50
evolution 13–14
exclusivity, Christian 115–129
exemplarism 57

faith 1, 16–19, 36, 75
Fall of Adam and Eve 23, 41–42,
43, 53; effects of 45–46, 47–48, 54,
55, 79; explanation of 49, 51, 52;
see also original sin
family, human 66
Faustus, Manichean Bishop 126, 128
filioque clause 39n17
foreknowledge, divine 5; and free will
84, 87–97
forgiveness 65
four-dimensionalism *see* time
free will: in Christ 71–72;
compatibilism 46–47, 48–49,
72, 78, 92, 94, 95–96, 109–110,
111; libertarianism 47, 51–53,

72, 78–80, 88–89, 92–94, 109,
111–112; value of 46, 51, 88; *see
also* foreknowledge; grace
Free Will Defense 59n35, 89
freedom, divine 4, 72

Genesis 13–14, 43
goodness, divine 3
government 123
grace 1, 19, 21, 48, 55, 66, 73, 75–
85, 92, 117–118, 122, 123, 127;
absent original sin 80–81; can be
lost 83; and free will 75–76, 78–80,
83; given equally 84; given only to
some 81–82; not certain 83–84;
without works 82–83
Great Schism 15, 27n35
greatness, divine 2
grounding principle 93, 94

happiness 65, 67, 81, 98, 99, 106,
115, 119, 128
heaven 98, 103, 107, 115, 128; proof
of 99; life in 108
hell 82, 103, 107, 109–112, 115, 118;
purpose of 110–111
heresies: regarding the Incarnation
60–61, 68–69; regarding the Trinity
15, 30; *see also* Albigensianism;
Arianism; Donatism; Manicheanism;
Pelagianism; social trinitarianism
heretics: definition of 120; treatment
of 119, 122–124
Hitler 119
hope 99
hylomorphism of human person
102–103, 106; *see also* Aristotle;
person, human

illumination, divine 9–10, 11, 36
immutability, divine 6–7
impassibility, divine 7
impatience, the first sin 52
Incarnation 8, 16, 18, 19, 21, 51,
53, 60–74, 101, 115, 122, 128;
Augustinian theory of 63, 64,
67–68; coherence of 61–62, 68–74;
debt payment theory of 63, 65–67,
68, 69, 77; purpose of 55, 61,
62–68
infants 82, 112n3
infinity of the past 3, 17
isotemporalism *see* time

Printed in the USA
CPSIA information can be obtained
at www.ICGtesting.com
LVHW011920111023
760831LV00006B/240